MARVEL
COLOR YOUR OWN
DOCTOR STRANGE

FEATURING THE ARTWORK OF:

Frank Cho, Sal Buscema, Stuart Immonen, Leinil Francis Yu, Chris Bachalo, Tim Townsend, Al Vey, Mark Irwin, John Livesay, Jaime Mendoza, Victor Olazaba, Gene Colan, Tom Palmer, Dan Adkins, Skottie Young, Bret Blevins, Terry Austin, Mundelo, Mike Mignola, Chris Warner, Kevin Nowlan, Alvaro Lopez, Marcos Martin, Frank Cirocco, Dan Green, Frank Brunner, Paul Smith, Steve Leialoha, Ed McGuinness, Dexter Vines, Neal Adams, Mike Deodato, Jim Cheung, Mark Morales, Paul Renaud, Steve Ditko, Marie Severin, Herb Trimpe, John Romita Jr. & Klaus Janson

COLLECTION EDITOR: JENNIFER GRÜNWALD
ASSOCIATE EDITOR: SARAH BRUNSTAD
ASSOCIATE MANAGING EDITOR: KATERI WOODY
ASSOCIATE MANAGER, DIGITAL ASSETS: JOE HOCHSTEIN
EDITOR, SPECIAL PROJECTS: MARK D. BEAZLEY
VP, PRODUCTION & SPECIAL PROJECTS: JEFF YOUNGQUIST
SVP PRINT, SALES & MARKETING: DAVID GABRIEL
RESEARCH: JESS HARROLD
BOOK DESIGNER: JAY BOWEN

EDITOR IN CHIEF: AXEL ALONSO
CHIEF CREATIVE OFFICER: JOE QUESADA
PUBLISHER: DAN BUCKLEY
EXECUTIVE PRODUCER: ALAN FINE

DOCTOR STRANGE CREATED BY STAN LEE & STEVE DITKO

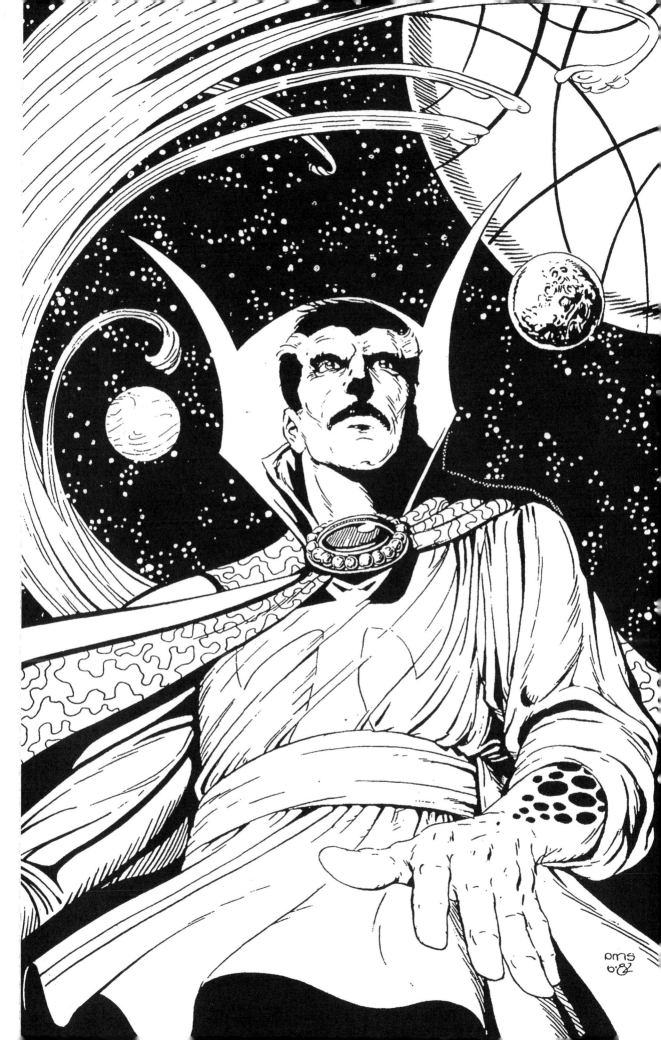

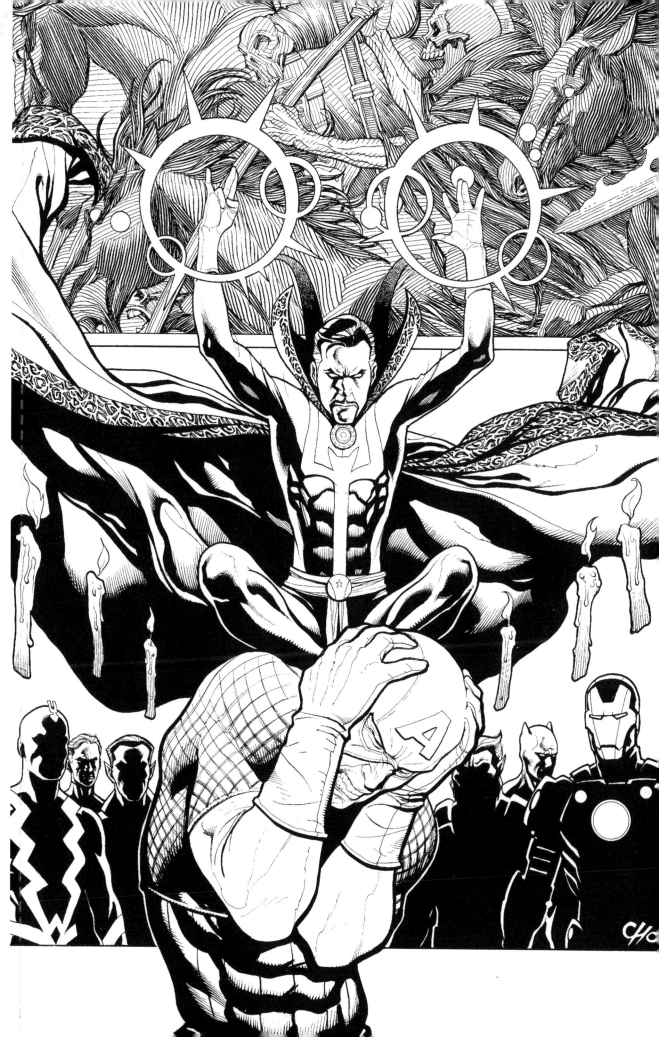

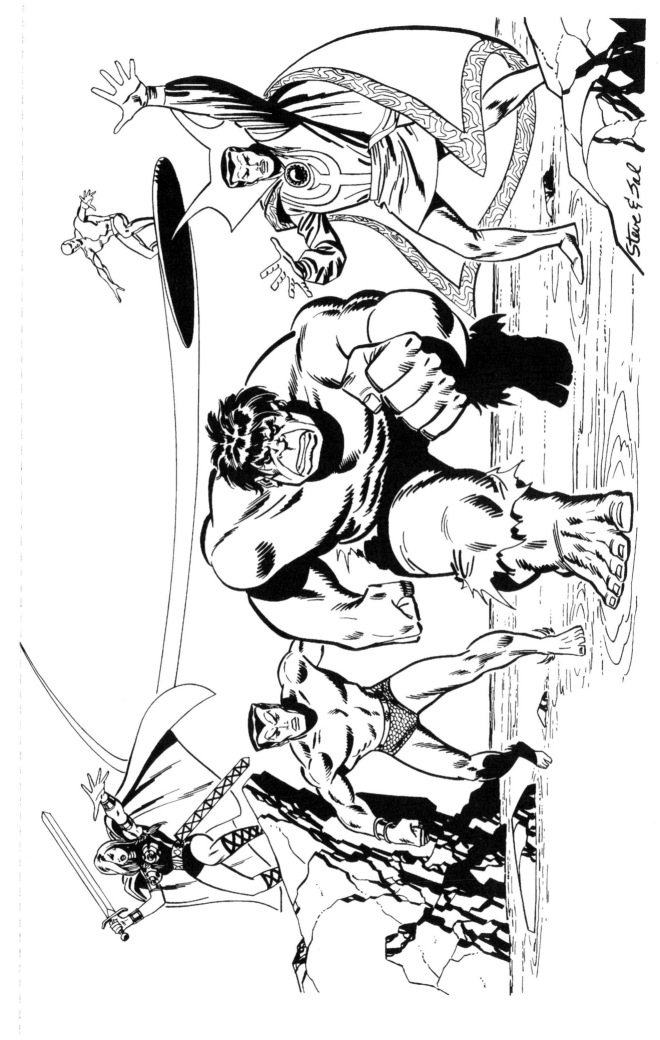

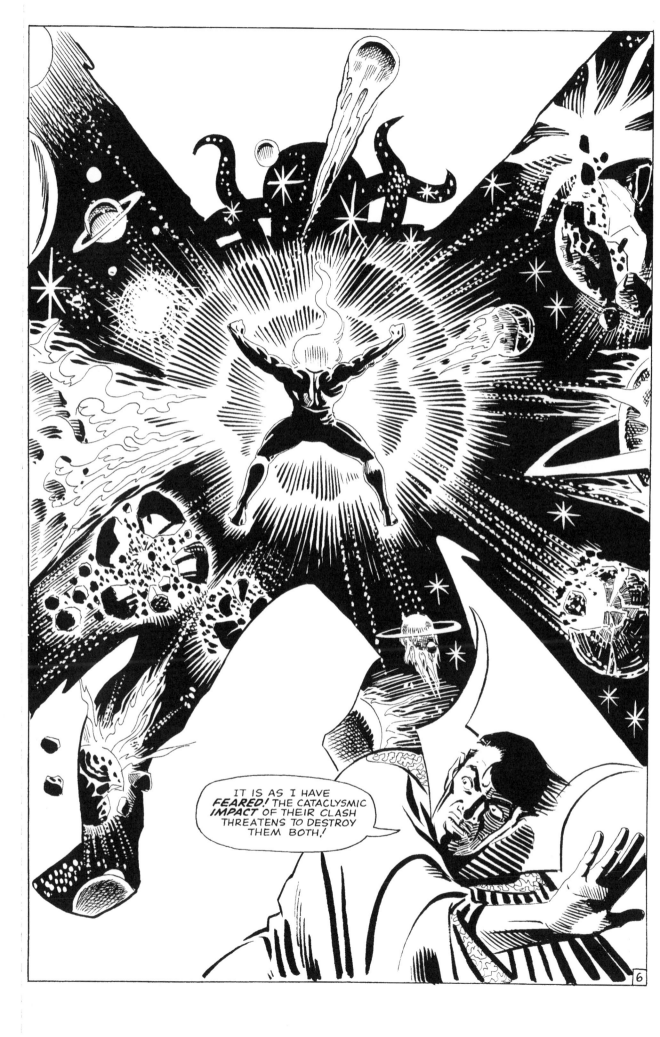

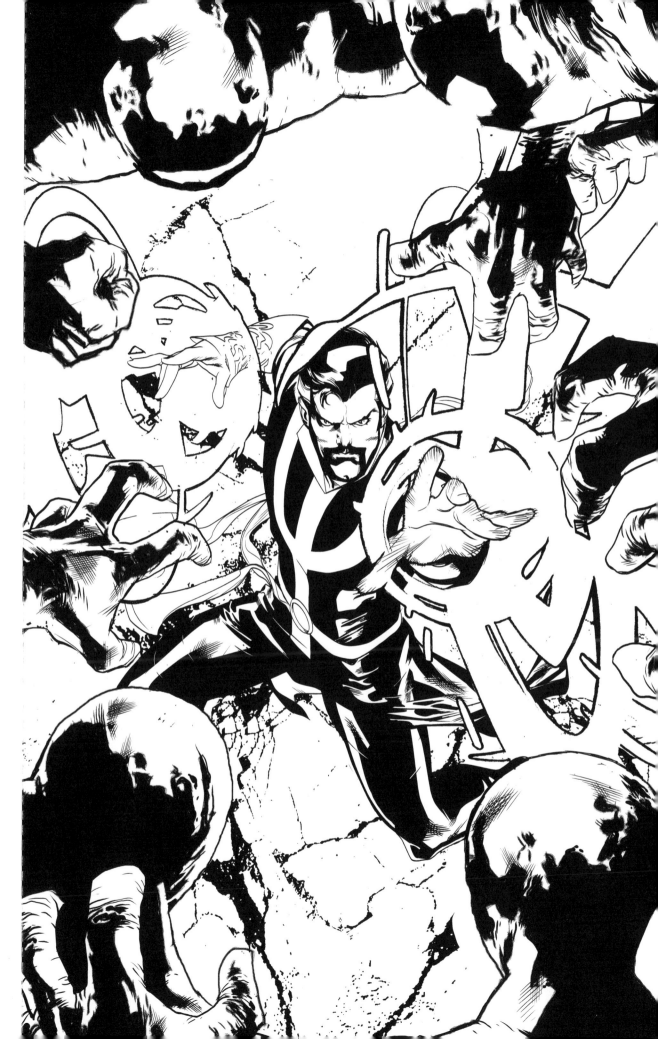

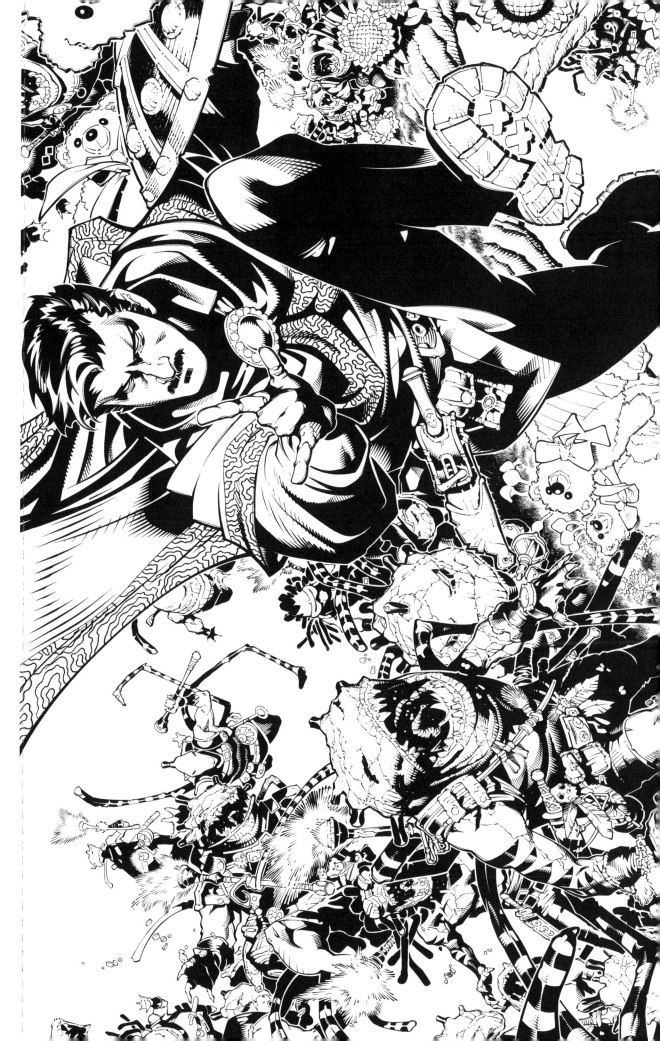

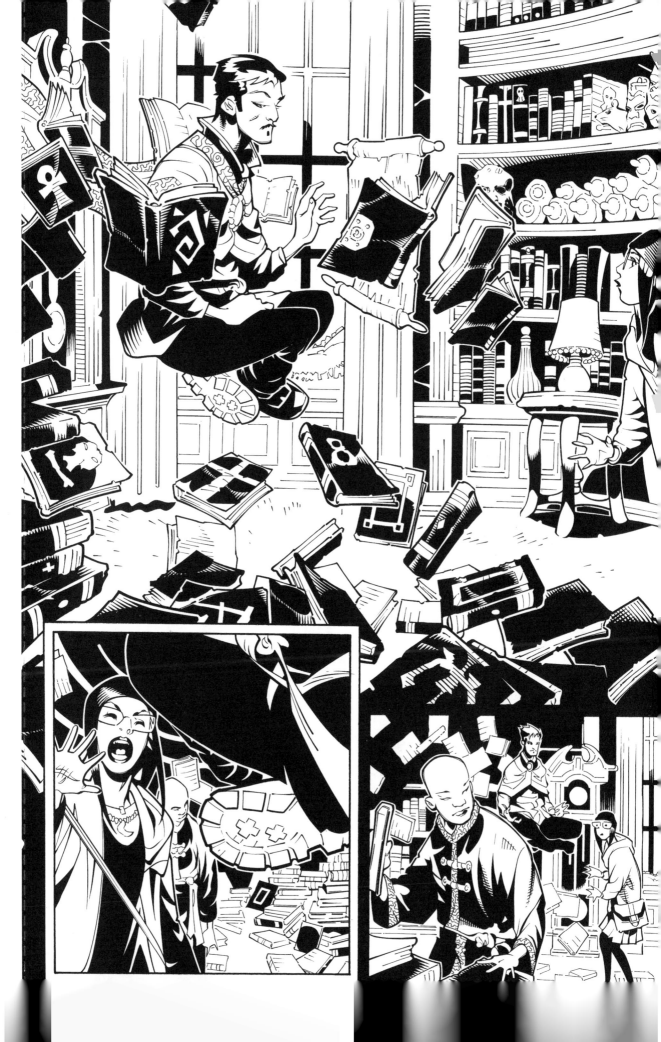

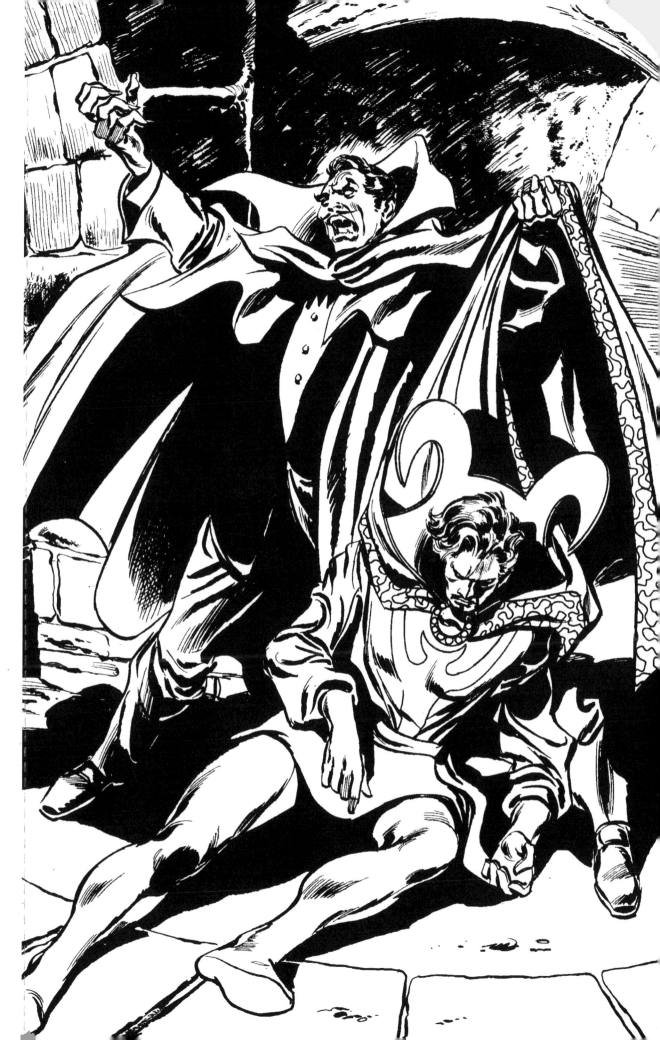

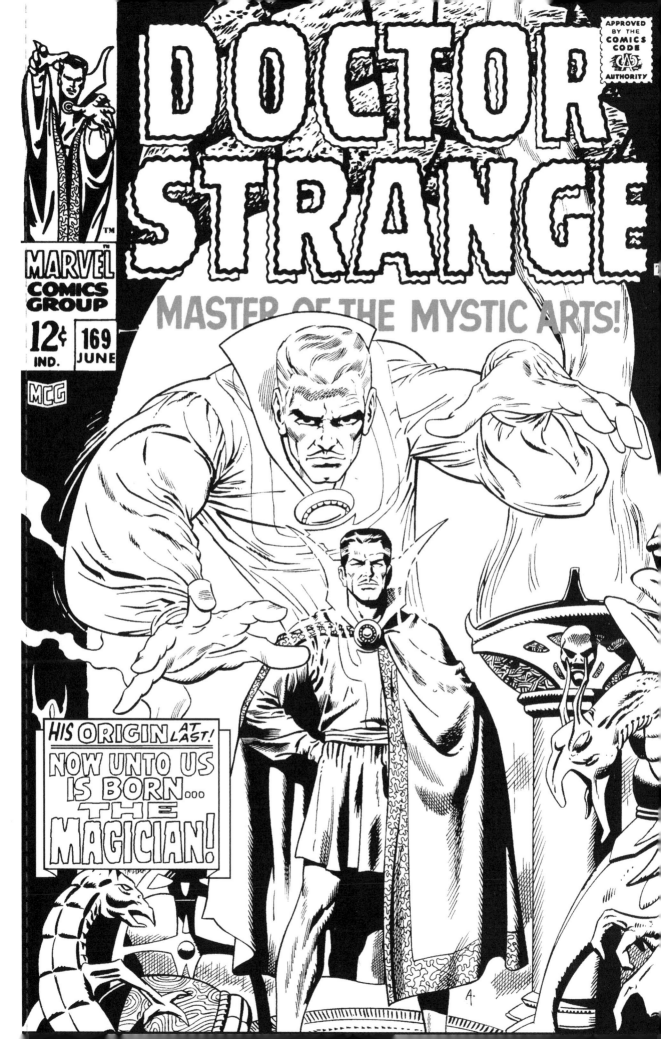

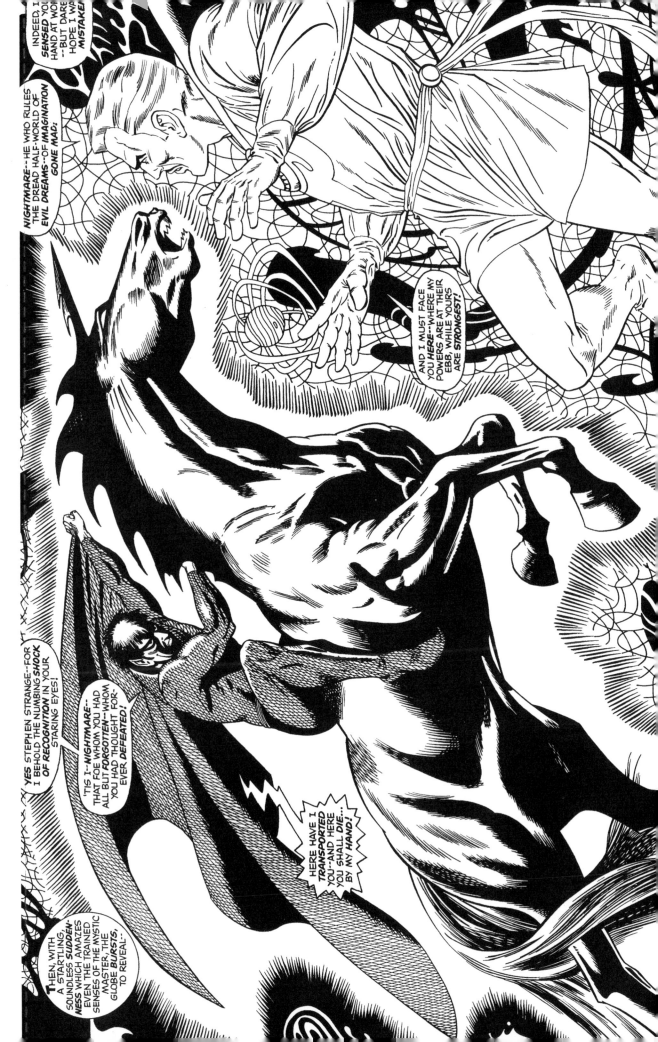

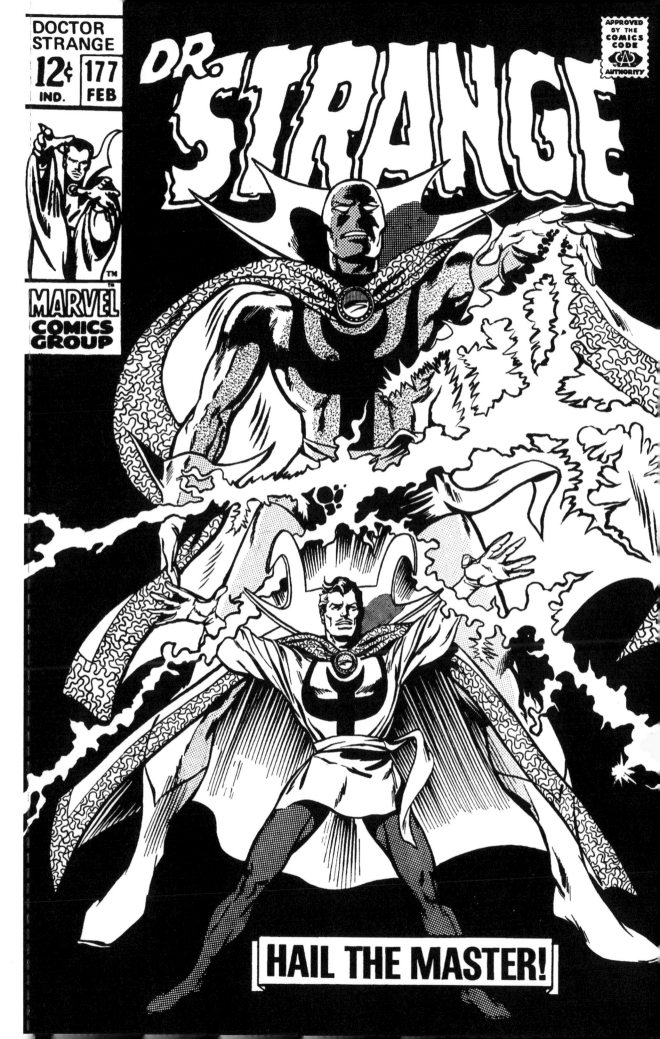

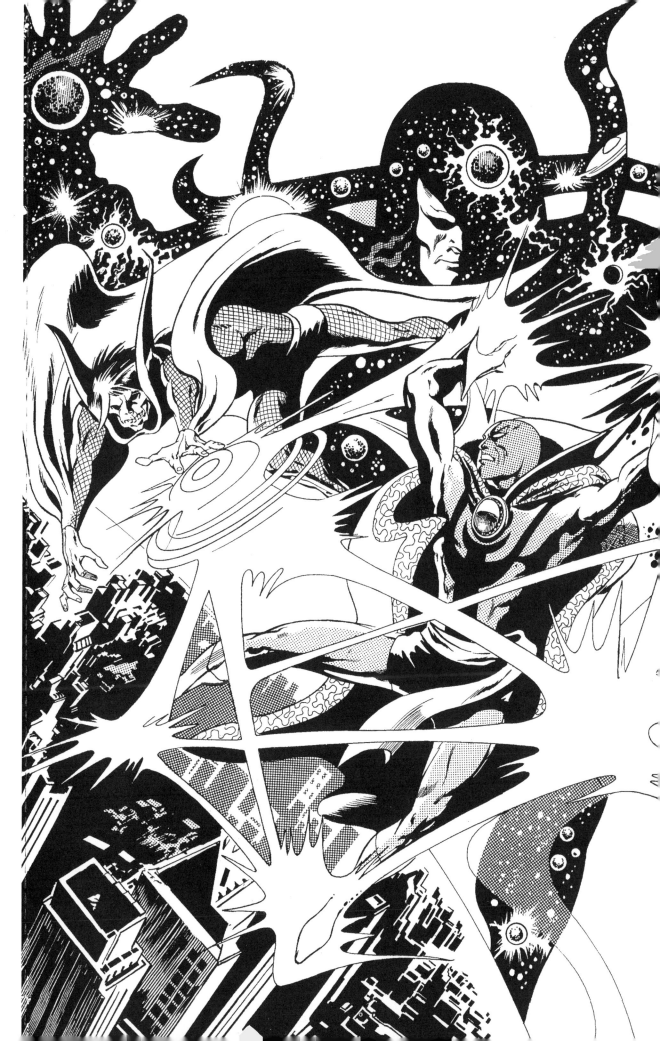

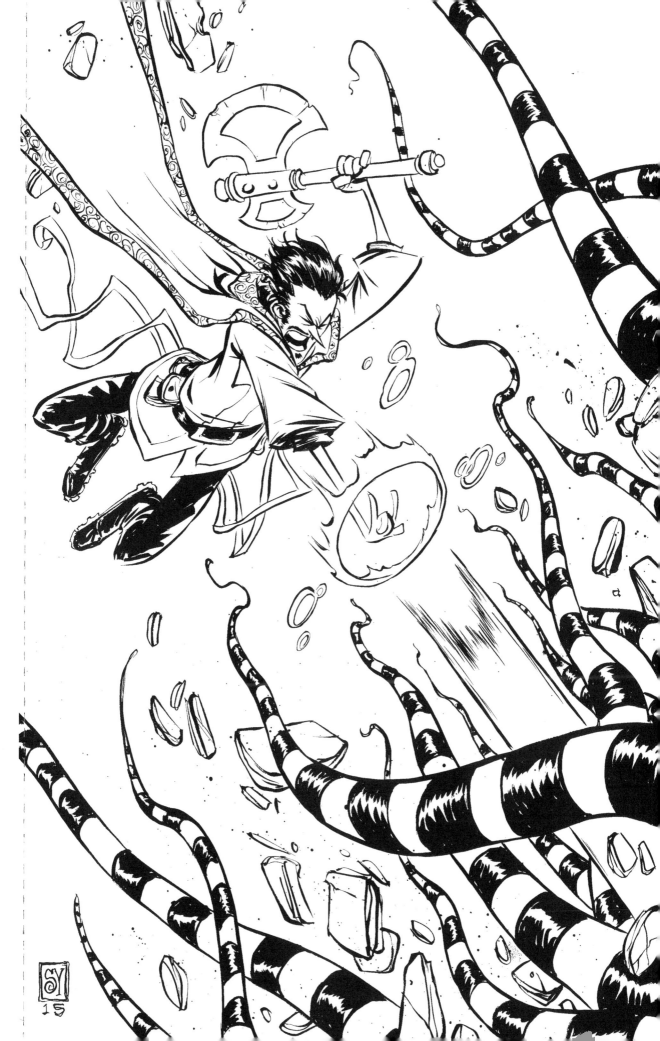

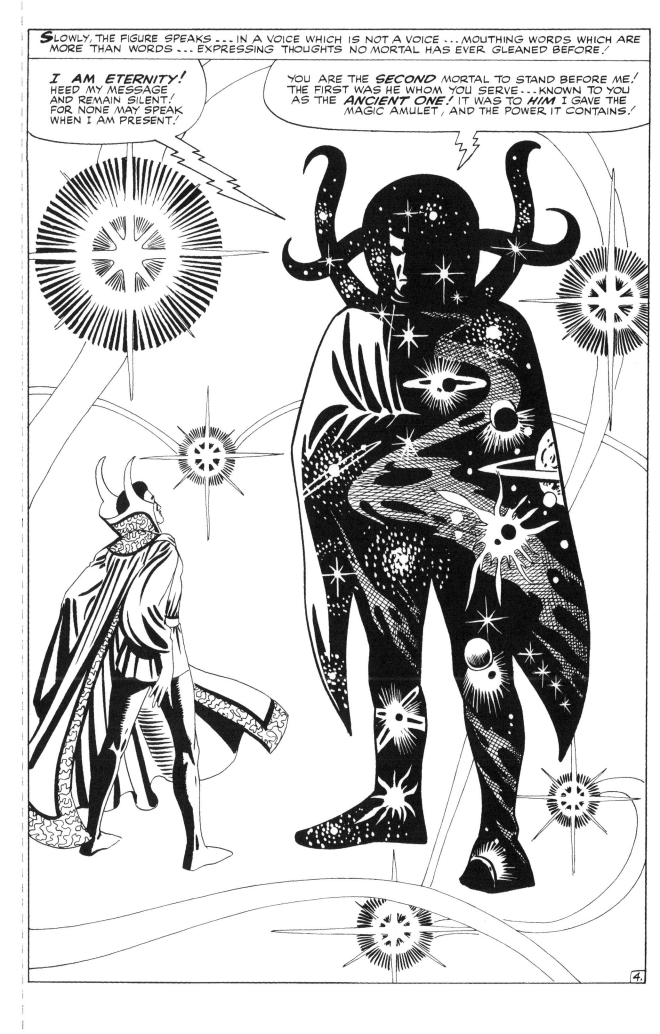

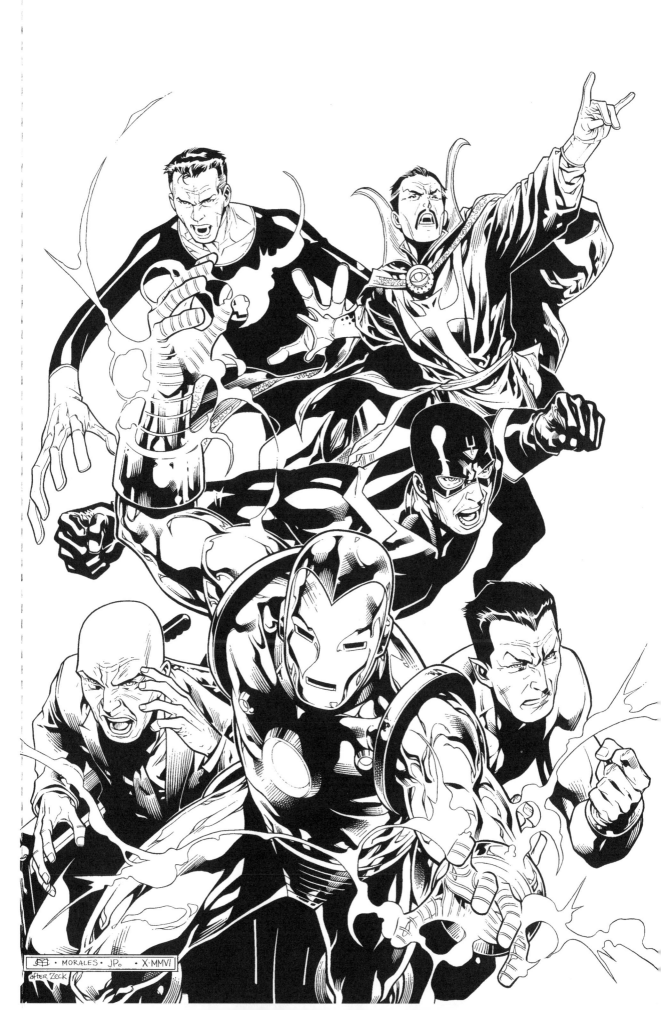

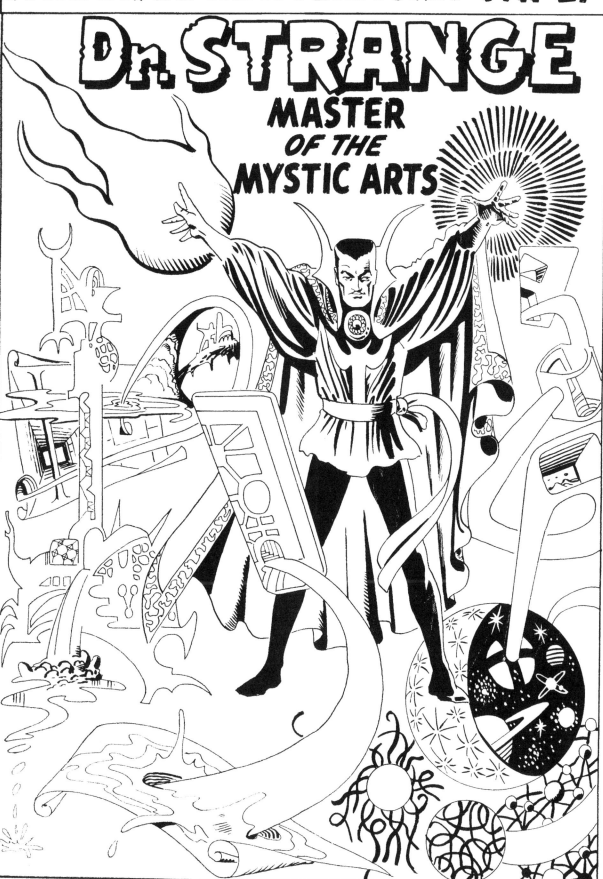

A MARVEL MASTERWORK PIN-UP

Dr. STRANGE
MASTER OF THE MYSTIC ARTS

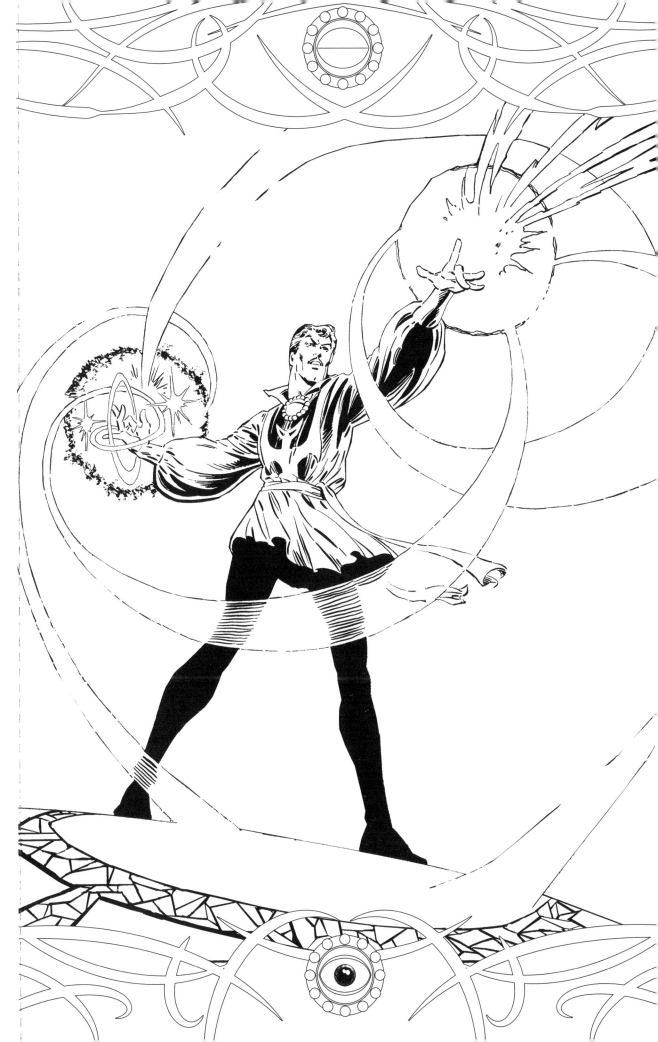

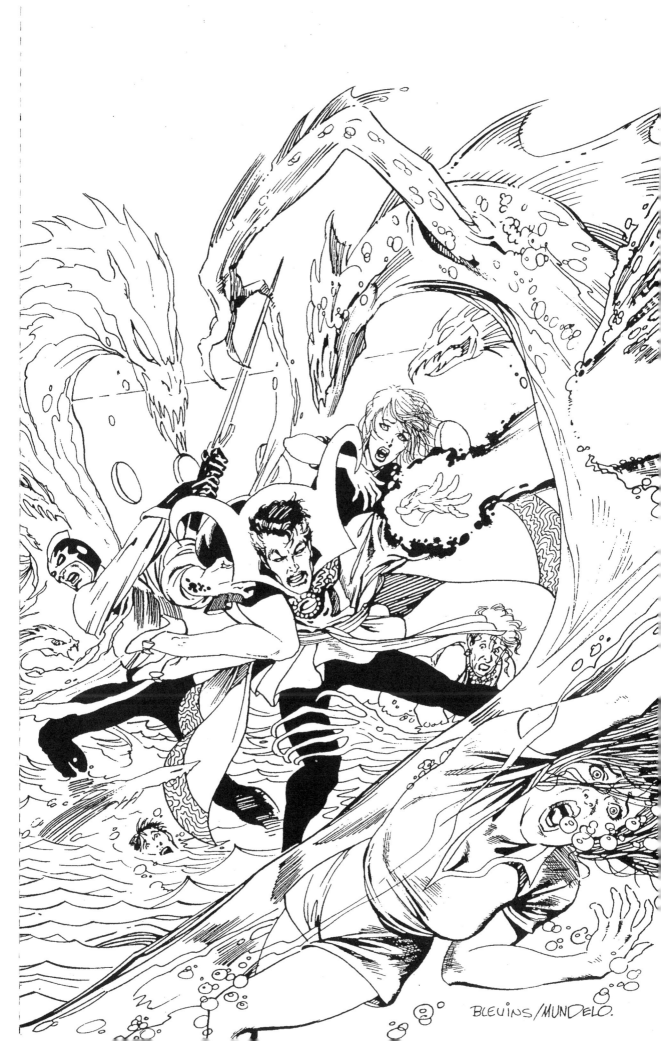

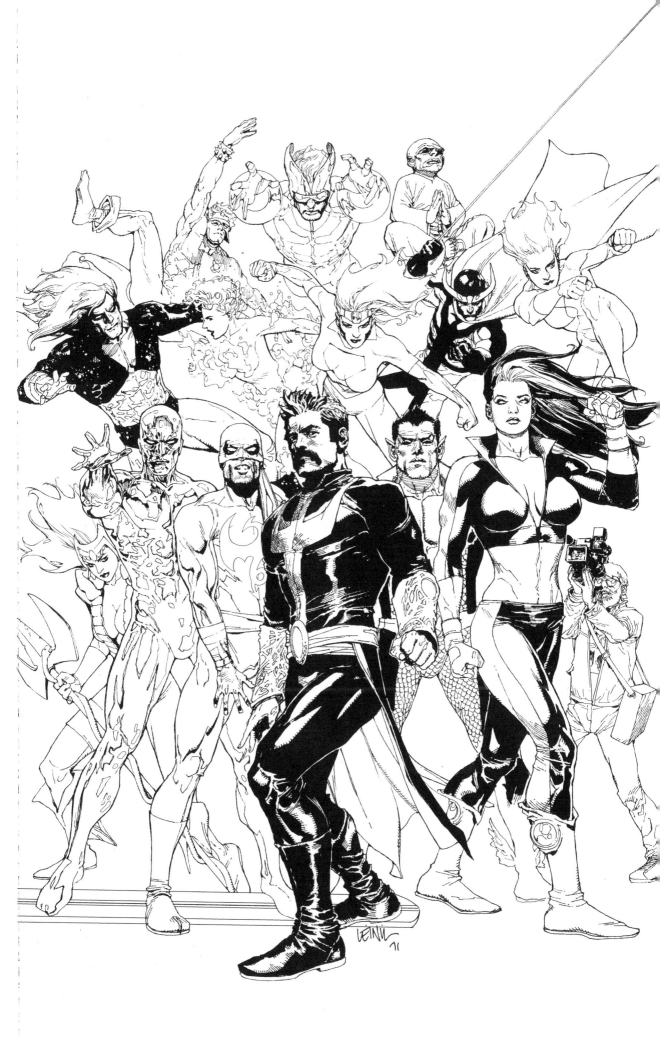

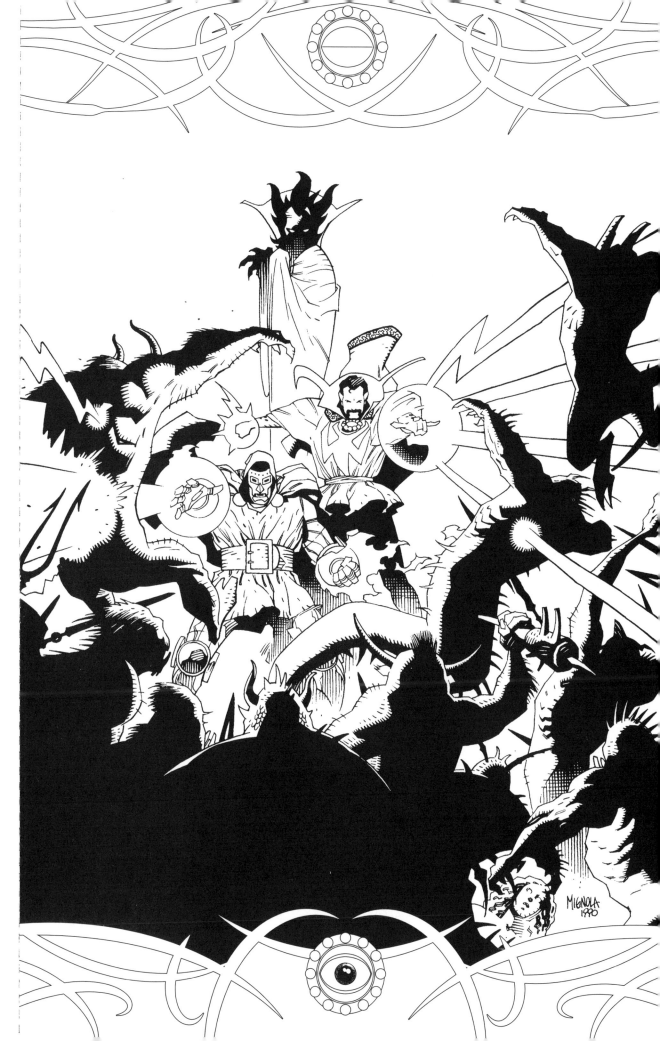

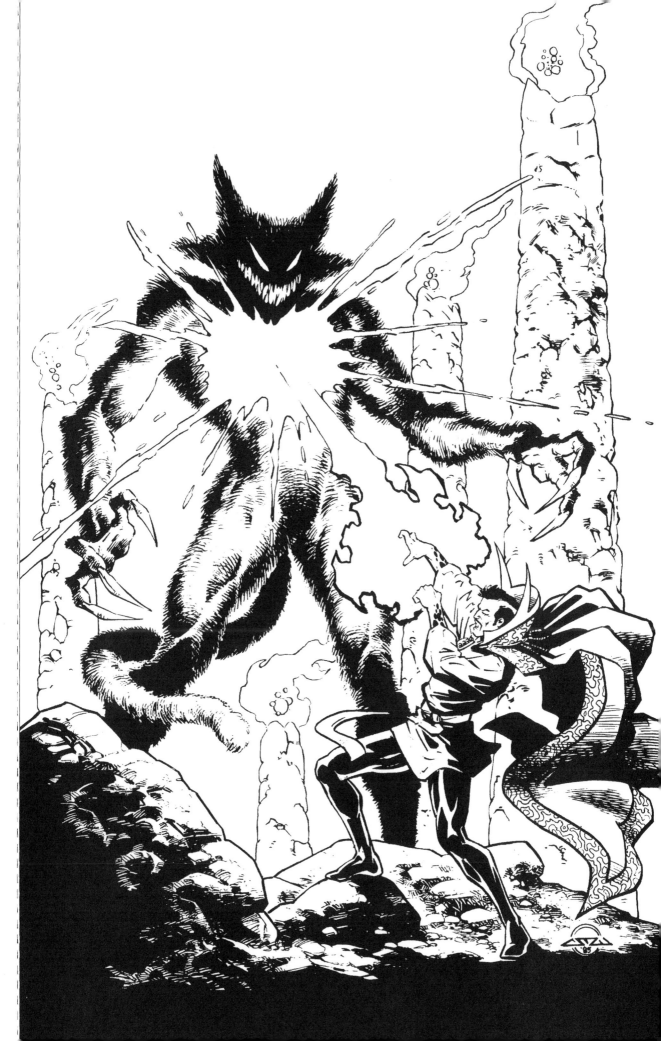

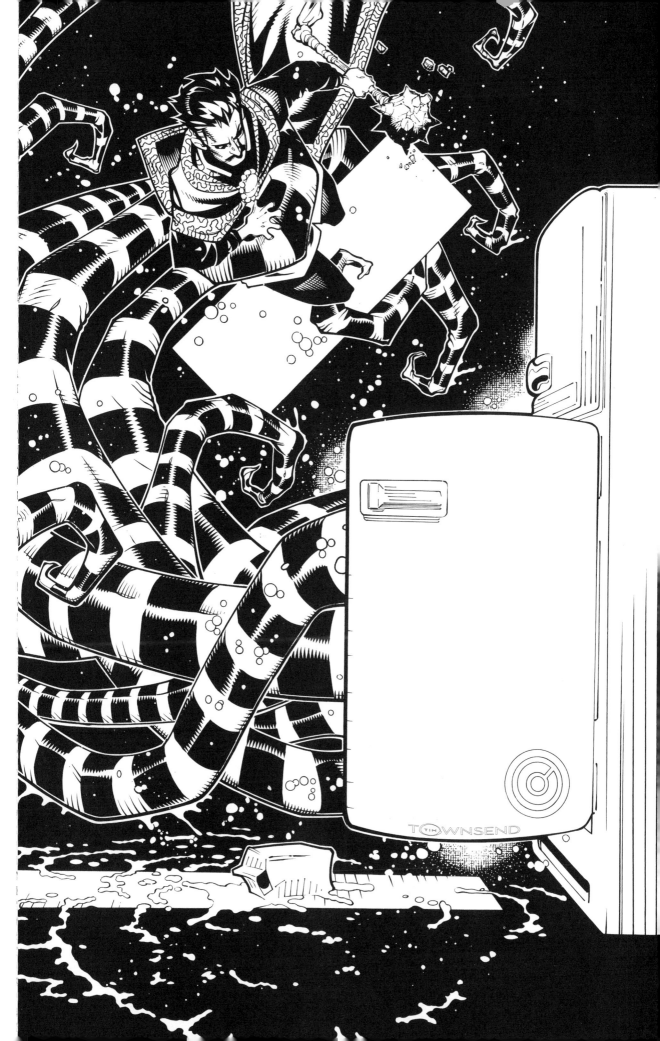

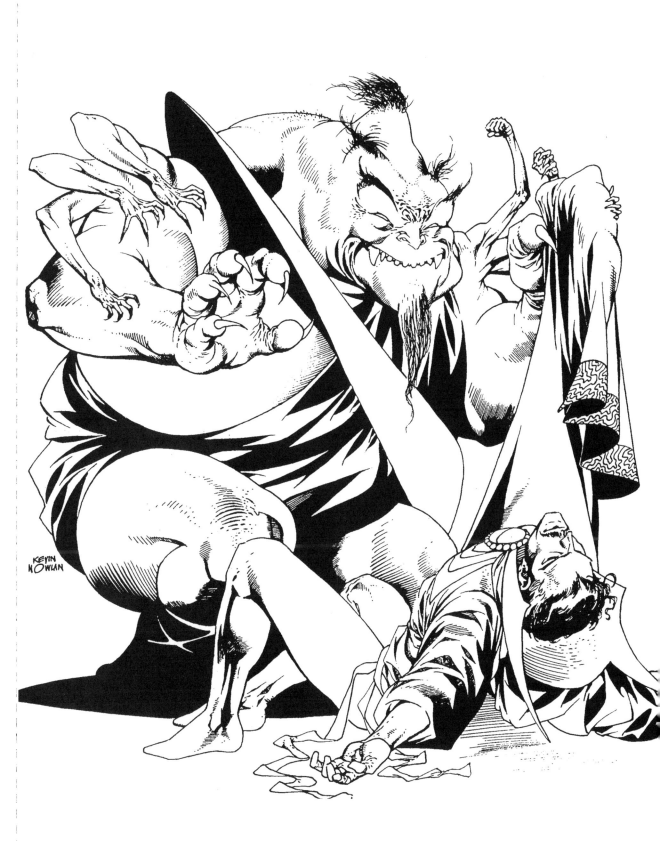

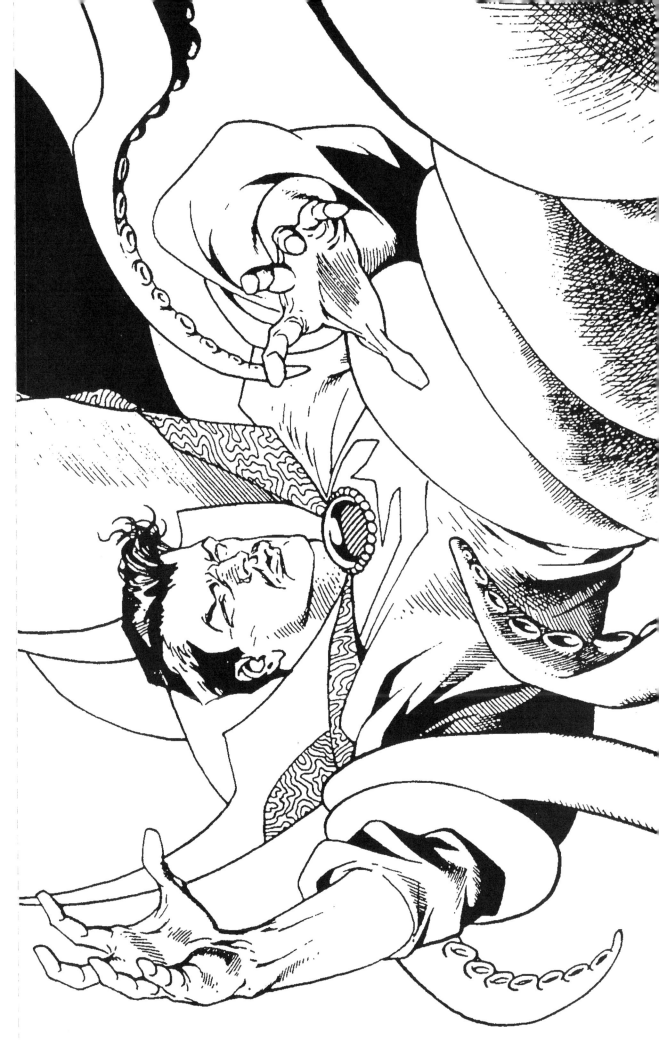

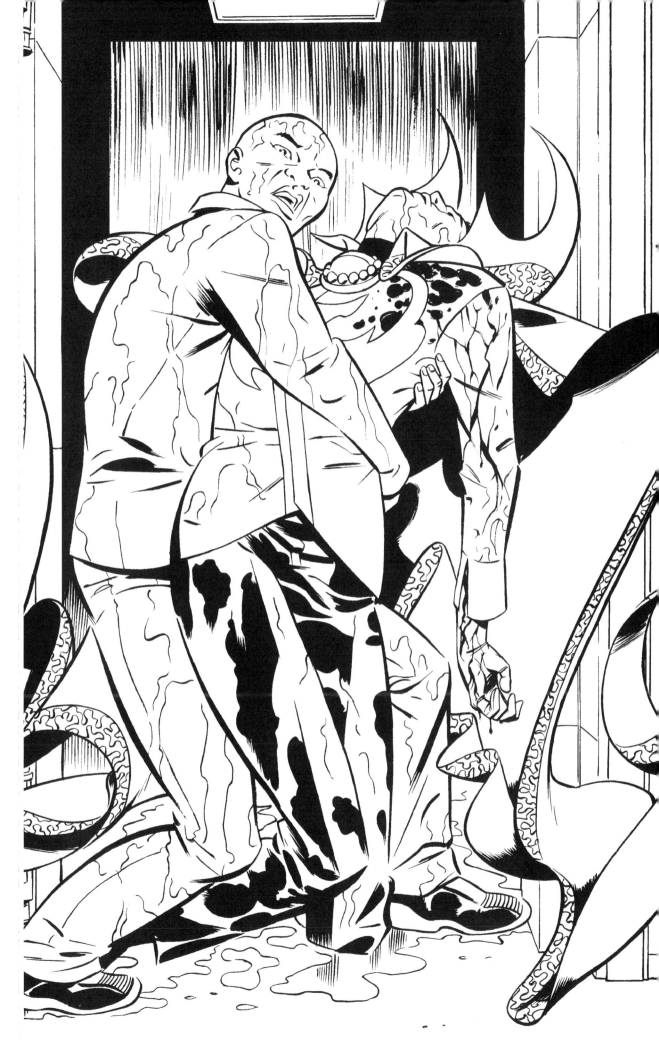

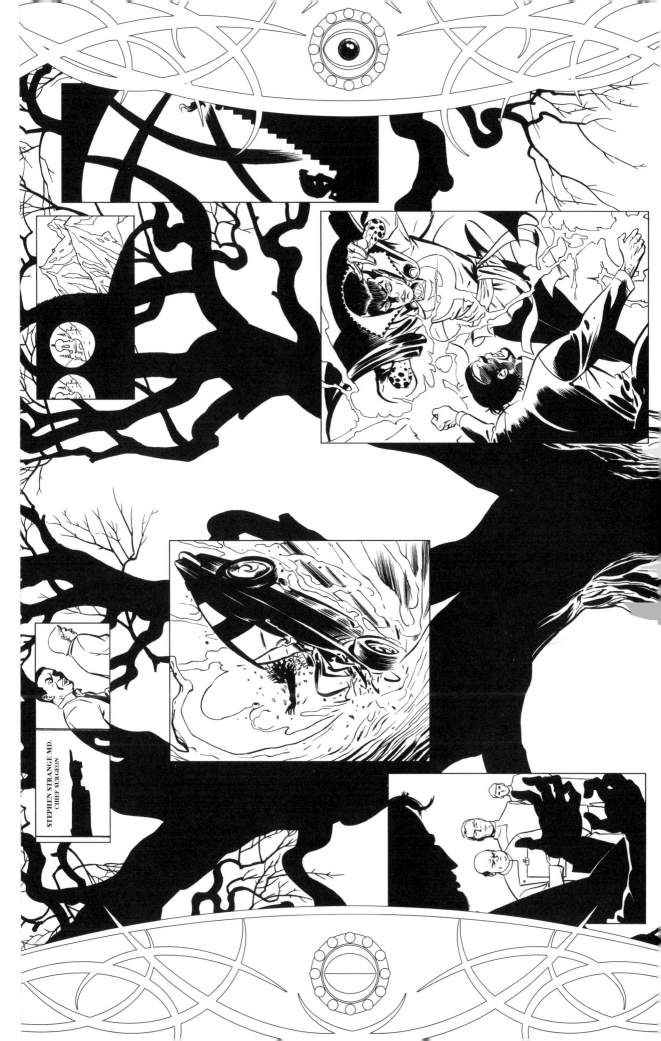

STEPHEN STRANGE M.D.
CHIEF SURGEON

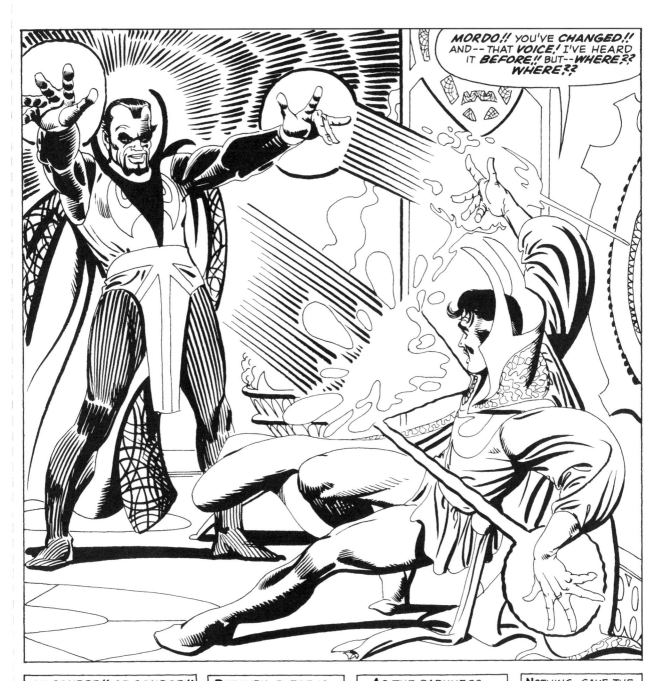

MORDO!! YOU'VE *CHANGED!!* AND -- *THAT VOICE!* I'VE HEARD IT *BEFORE!!* BUT -- *WHERE??* *WHERE??*

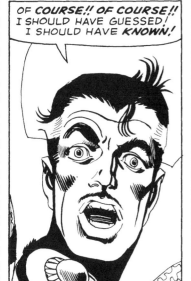

OF *COURSE!!* OF *COURSE!!* I SHOULD HAVE GUESSED! I SHOULD HAVE *KNOWN!*

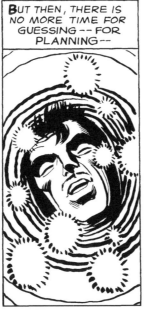

BUT THEN, THERE IS NO MORE TIME FOR GUESSING -- FOR PLANNING --

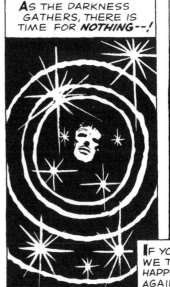

AS THE DARKNESS GATHERS, THERE IS TIME FOR *NOTHING --!*

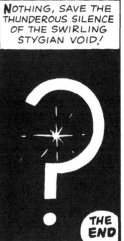

NOTHING, SAVE THE THUNDEROUS SILENCE OF THE SWIRLING STYGIAN VOID.!

THE END

IF YOU'RE AS ANXIOUS AS WE TO LEARN WHAT HAPPENS, MEET US HERE AGAIN NEXT ISH -- AND BRING YOUR AMULET!

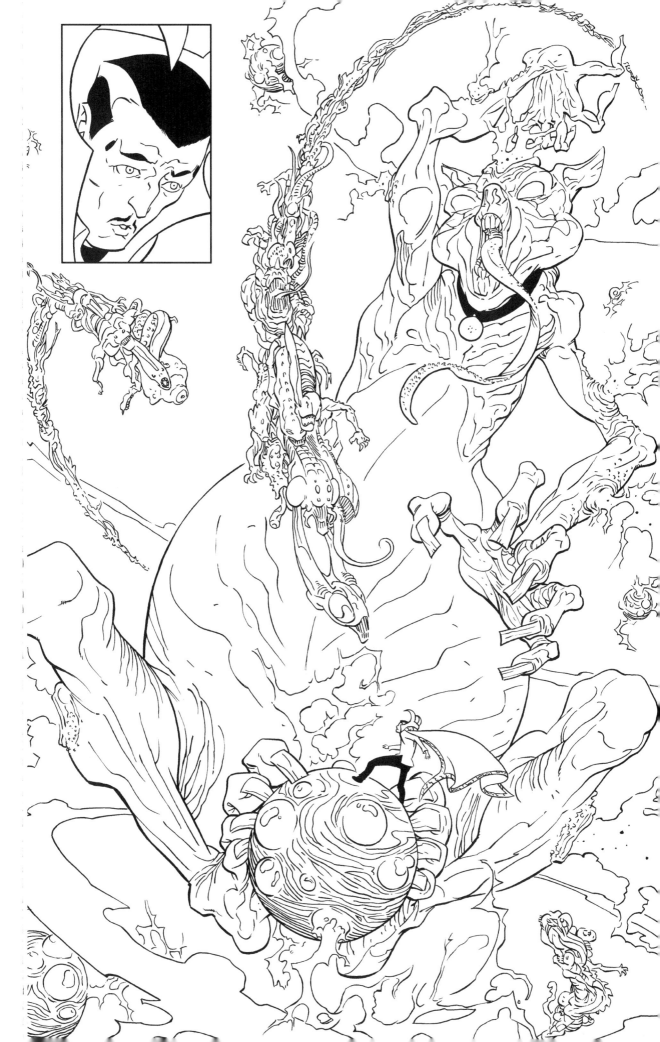

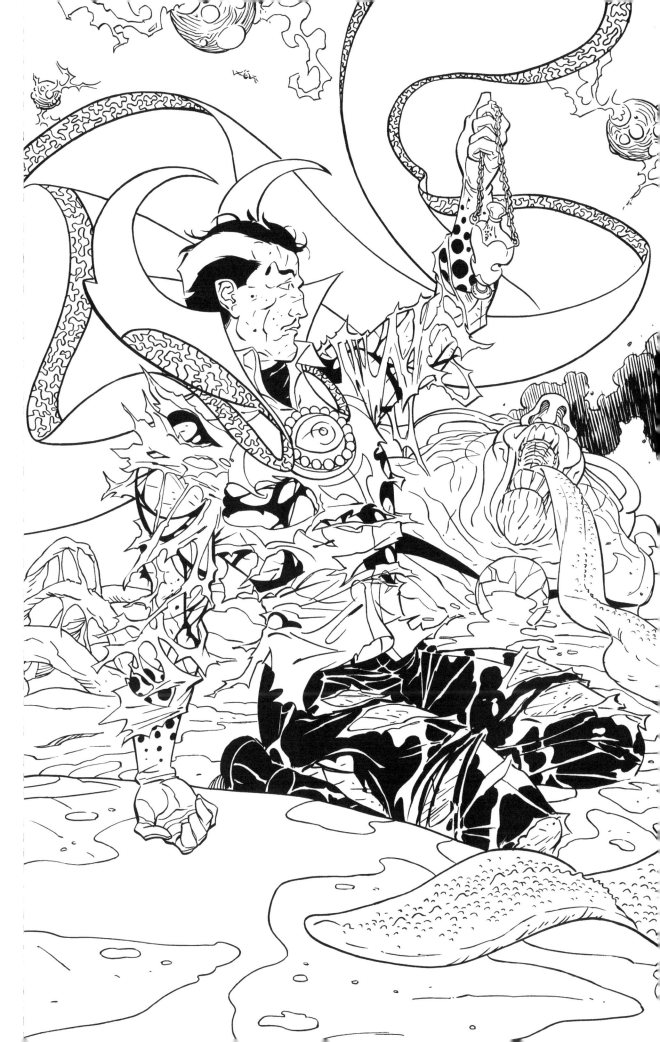

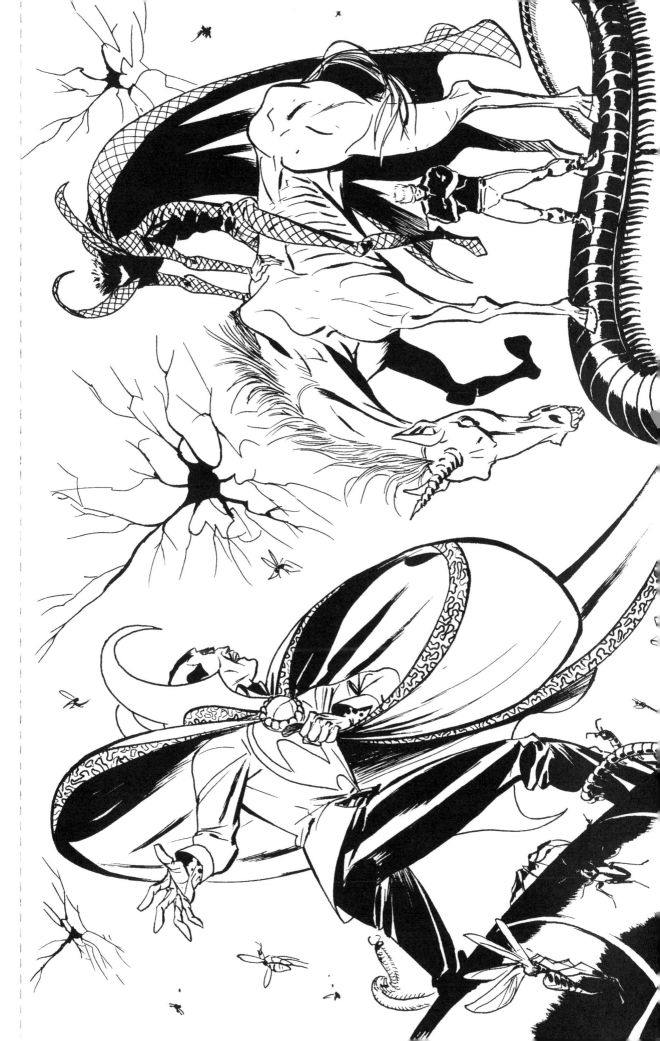

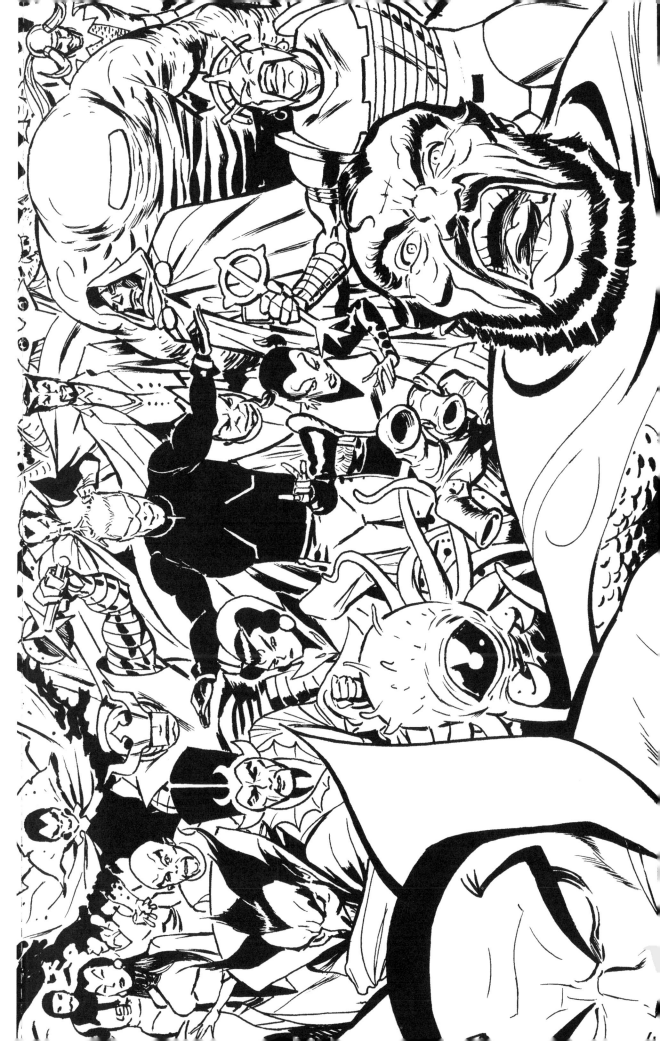

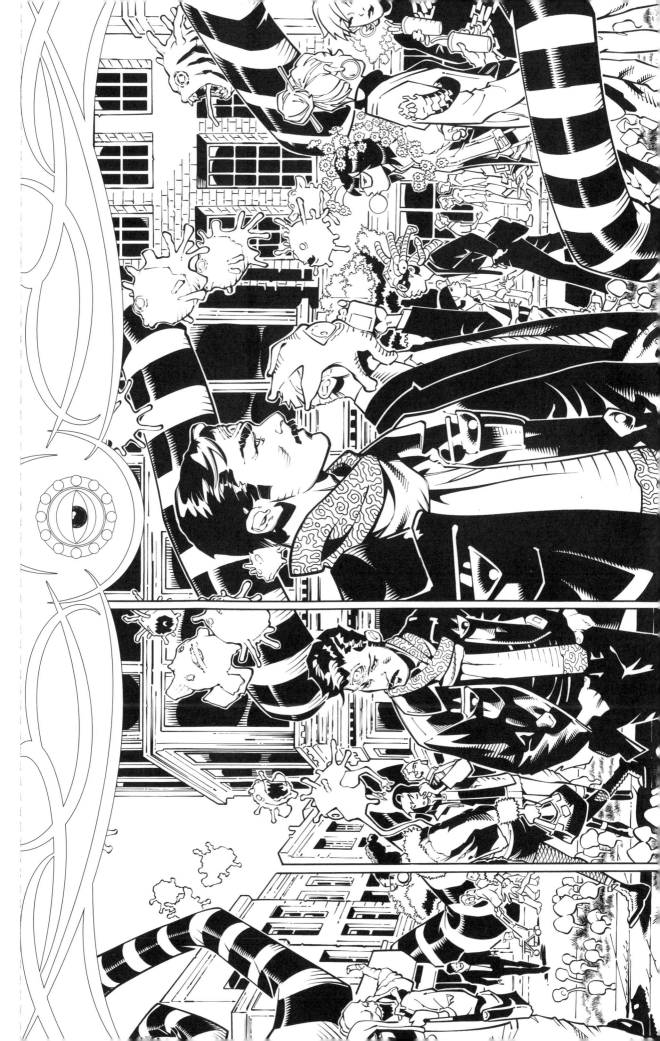

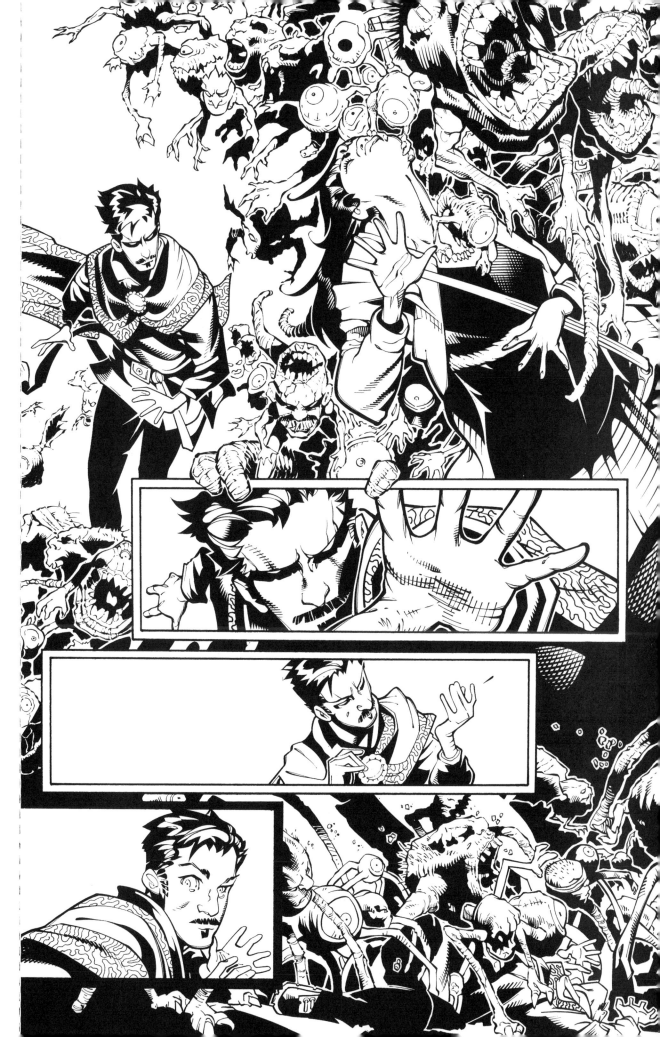

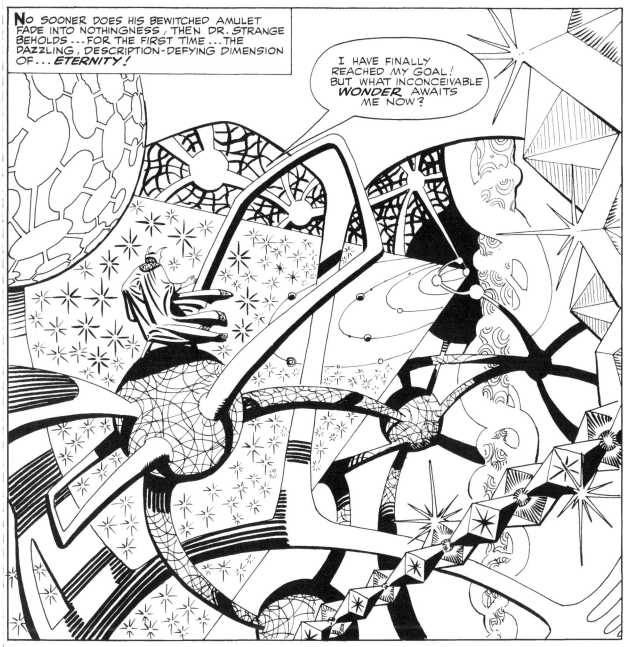

NO SOONER DOES HIS BEWITCHED AMULET FADE INTO NOTHINGNESS, THEN DR. STRANGE BEHOLDS...FOR THE FIRST TIME...THE DAZZLING, DESCRIPTION-DEFYING DIMENSION OF...*ETERNITY!*

I HAVE FINALLY REACHED MY GOAL! BUT WHAT INCONCEIVABLE *WONDER* AWAITS ME NOW?

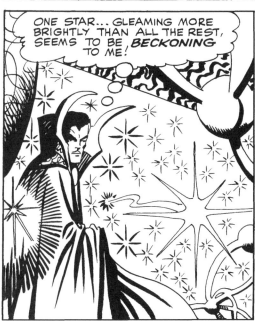

ONE STAR... GLEAMING MORE BRIGHTLY THAN ALL THE REST, SEEMS TO BE *BECKONING* TO ME!

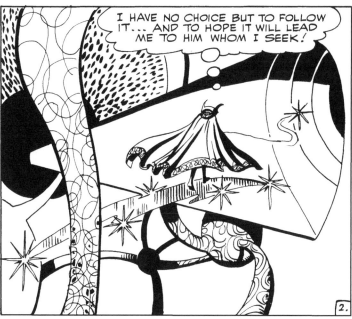

I HAVE NO CHOICE BUT TO FOLLOW IT... AND TO HOPE IT WILL LEAD ME TO HIM WHOM I SEEK!

2.

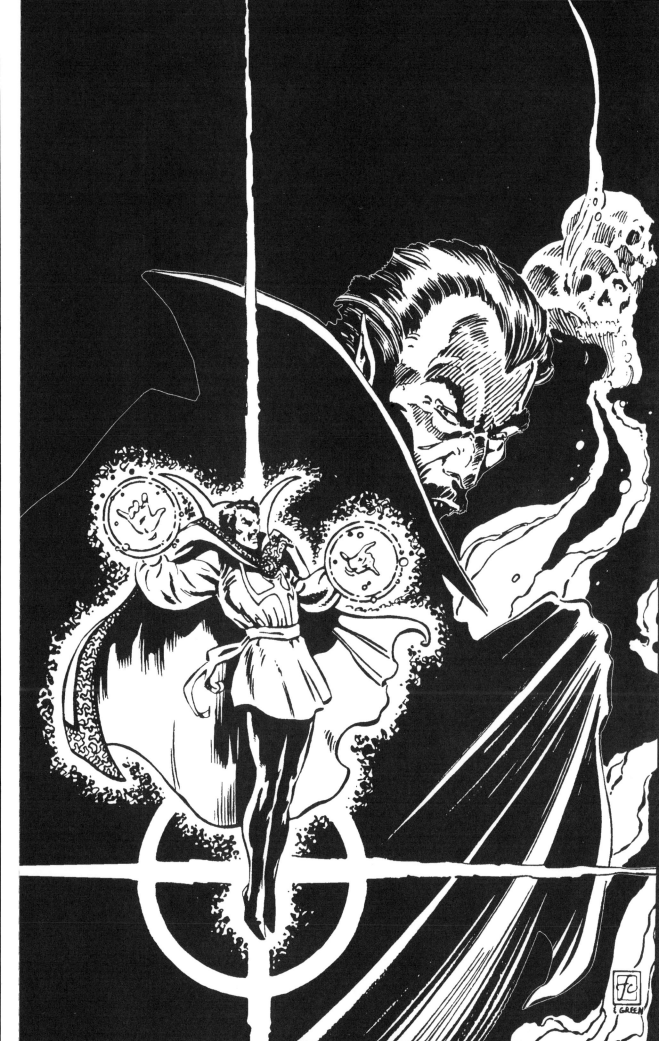

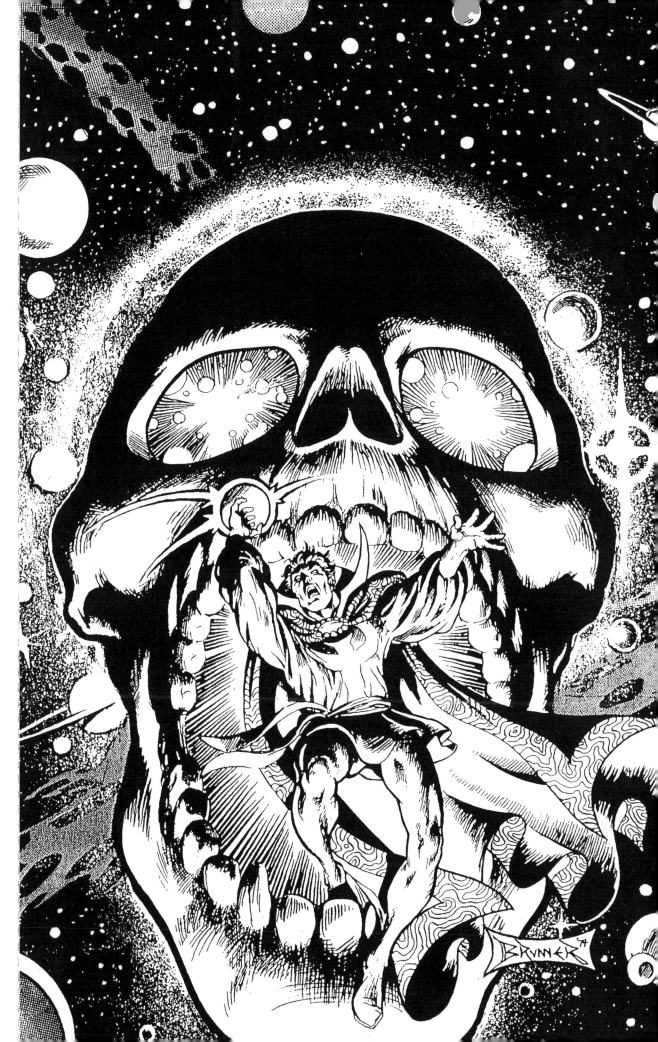

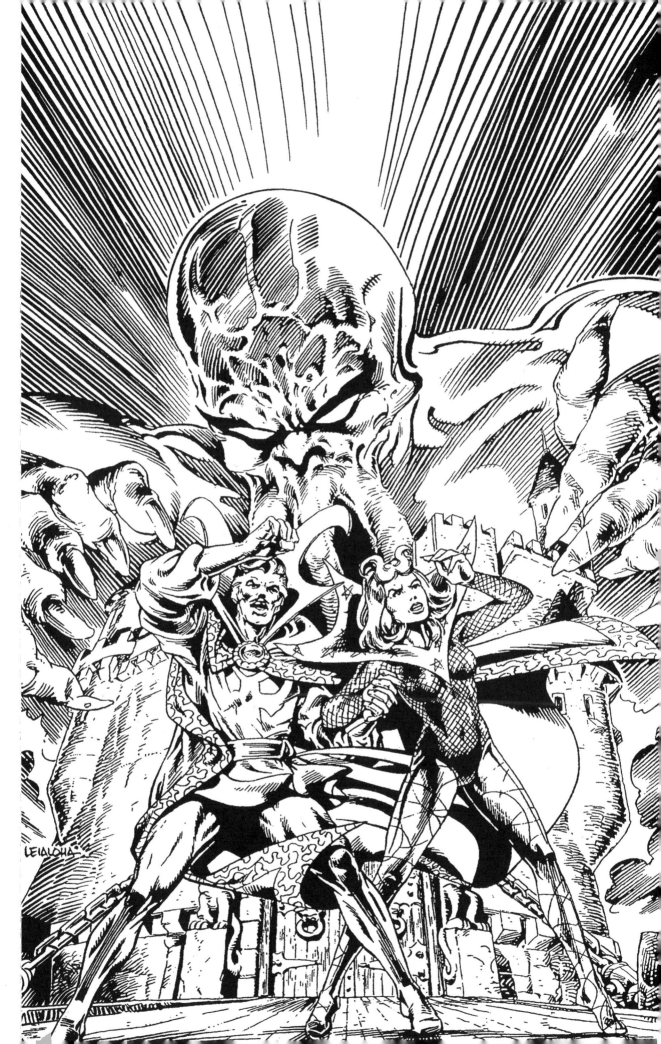

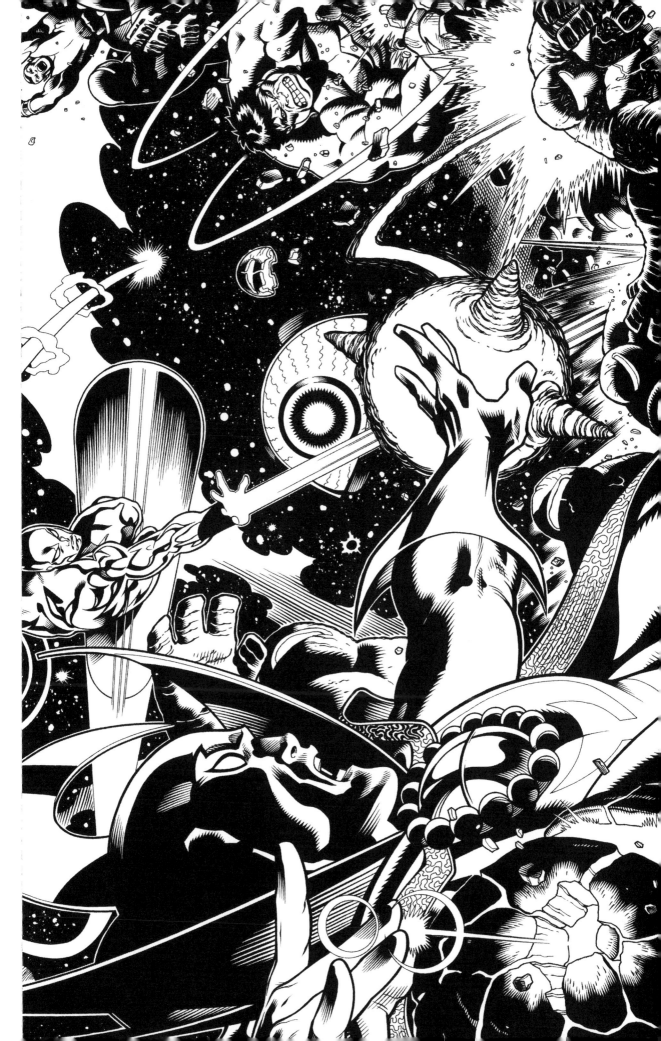

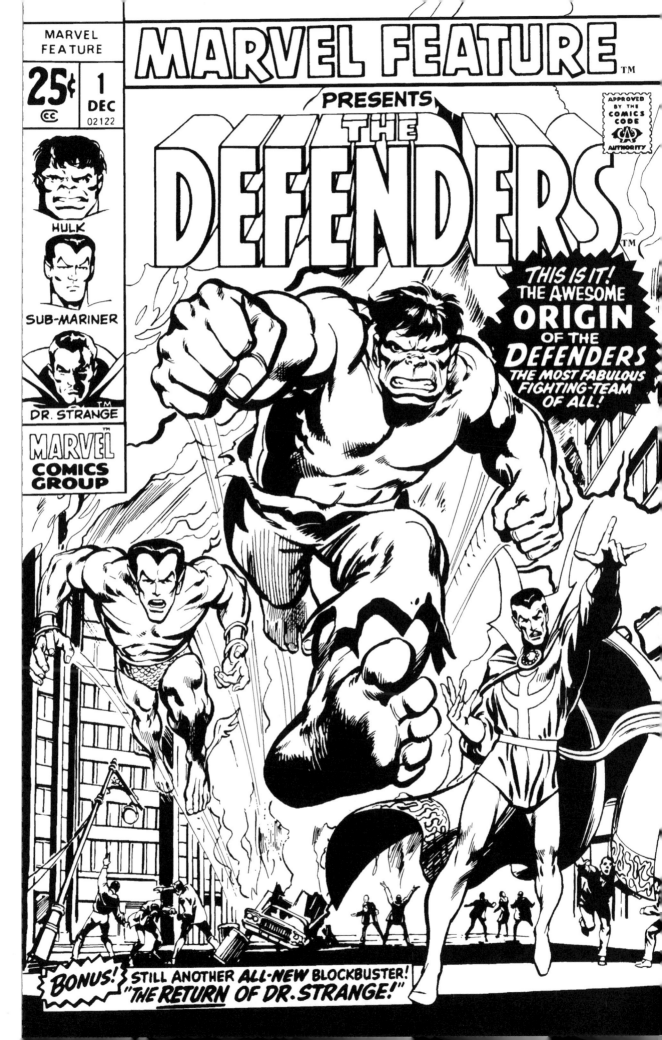

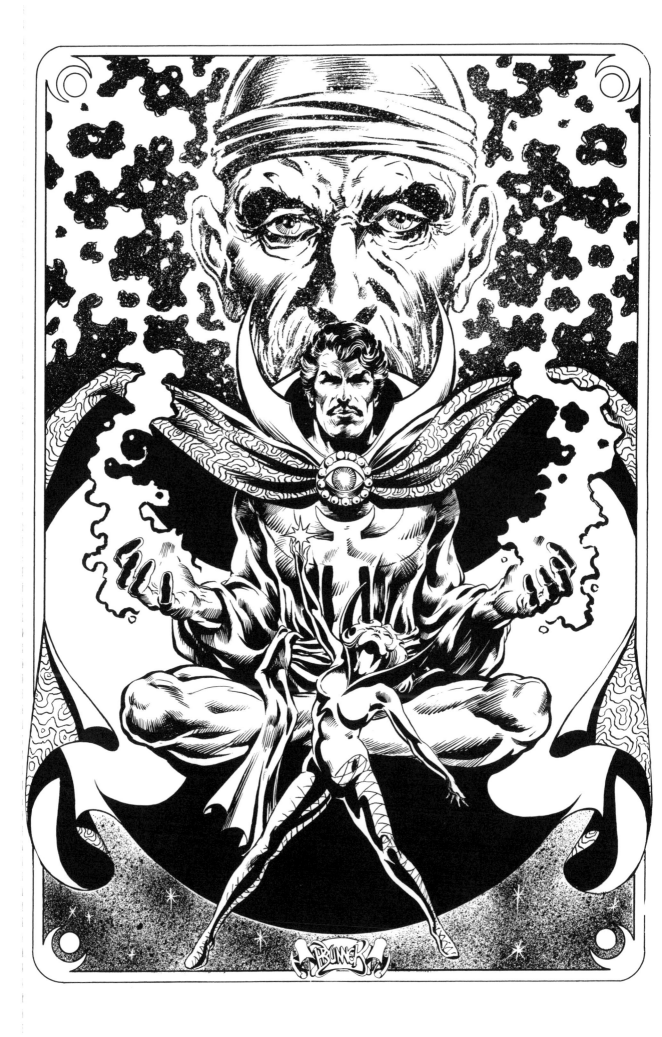

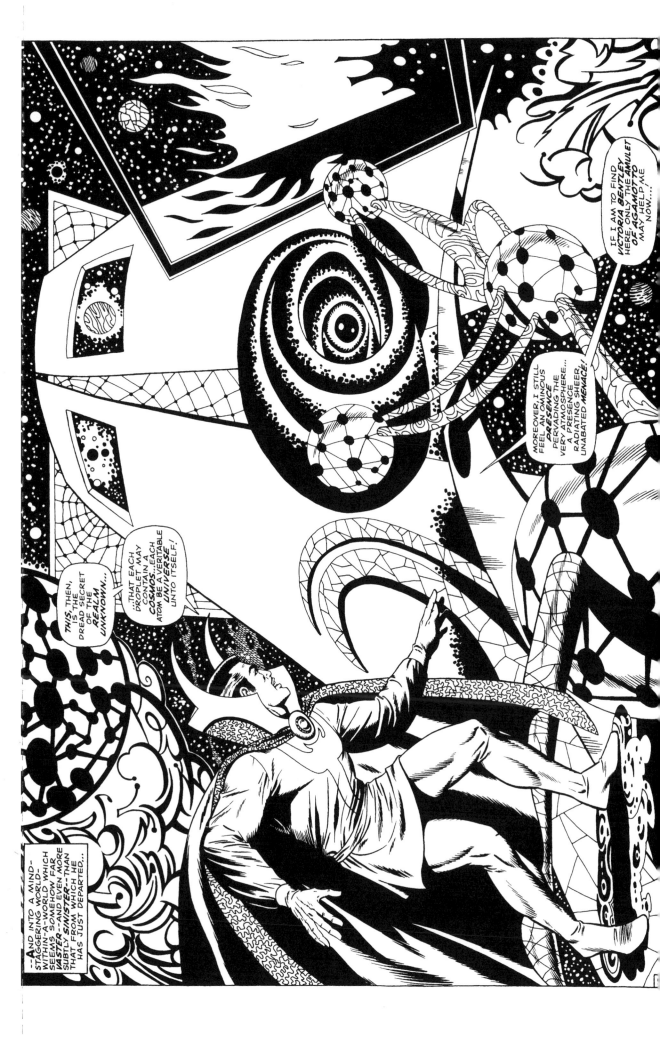

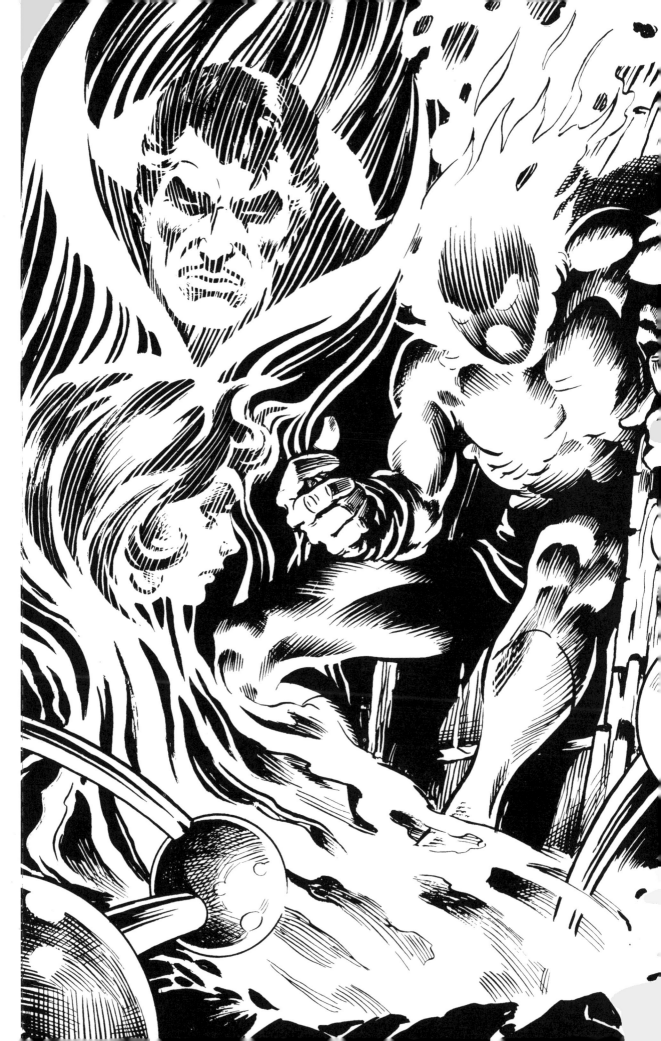

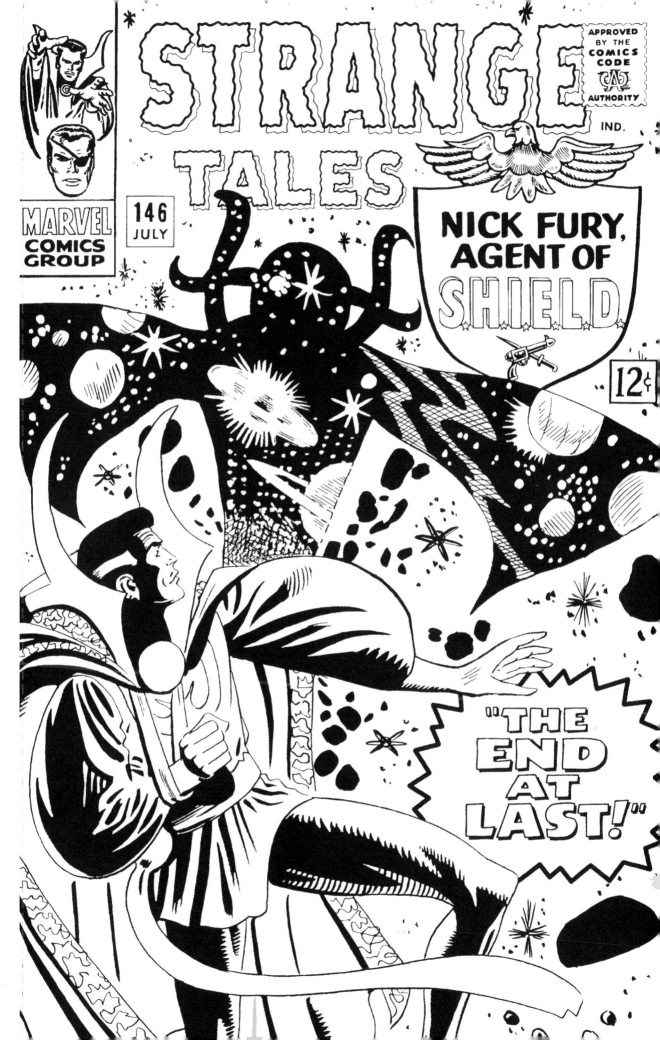

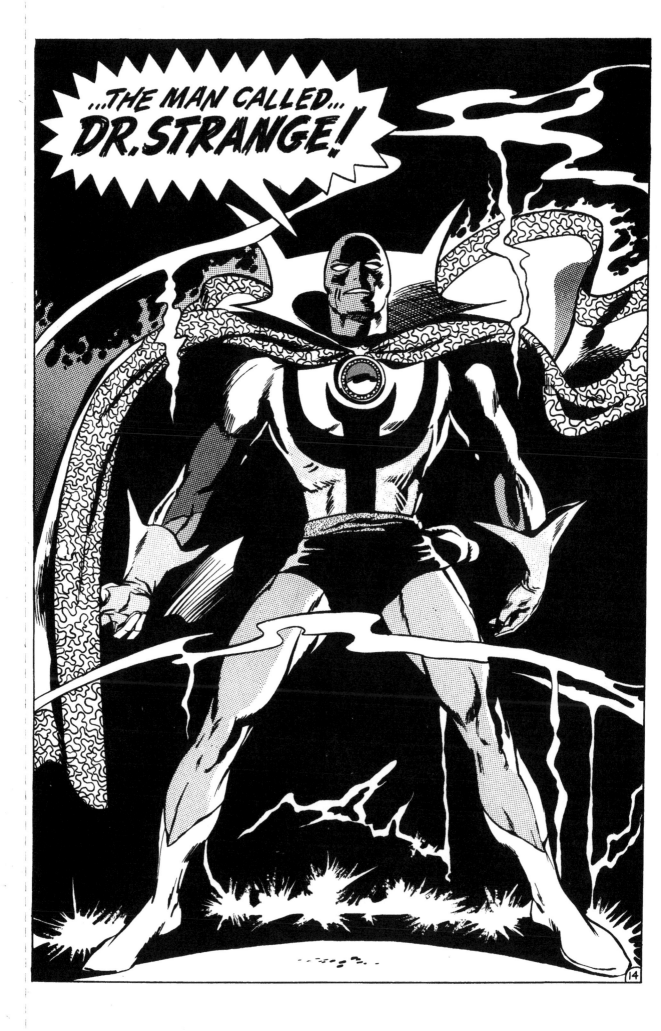

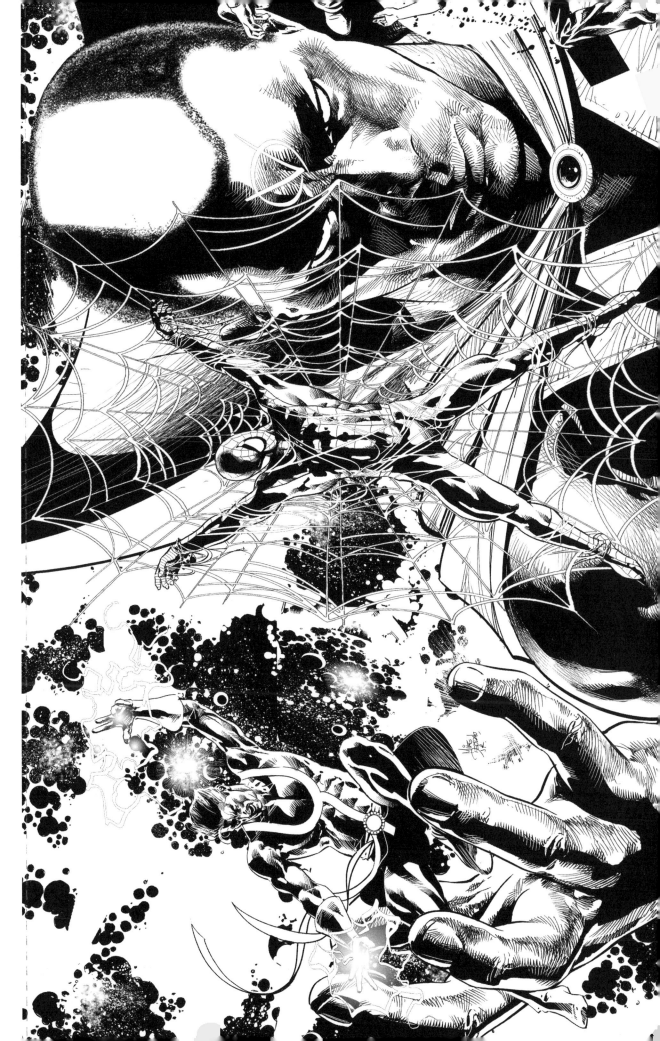

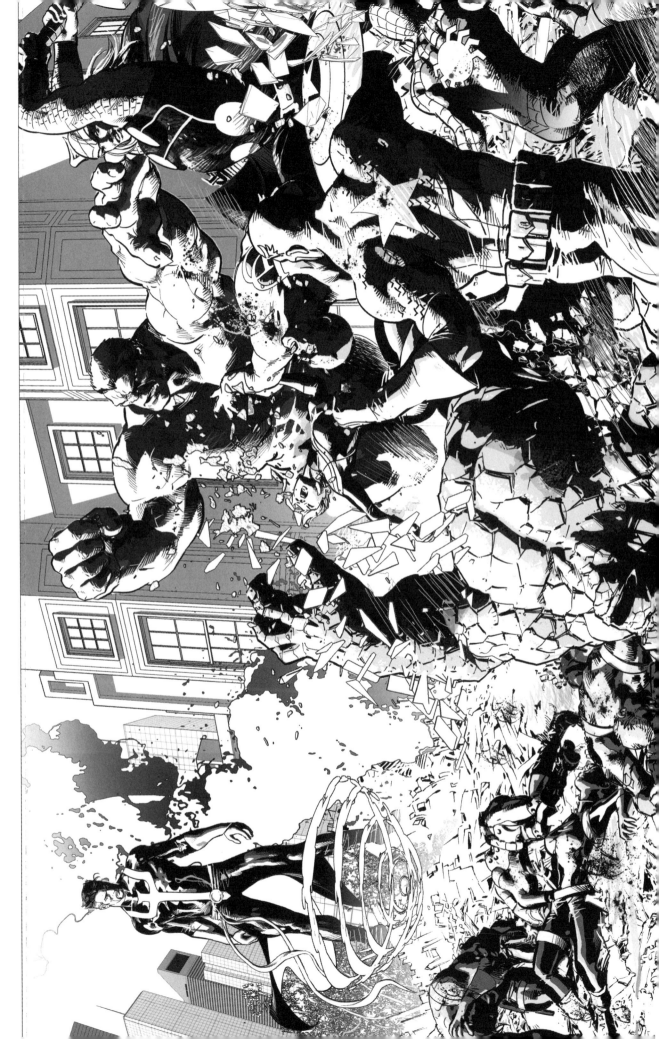

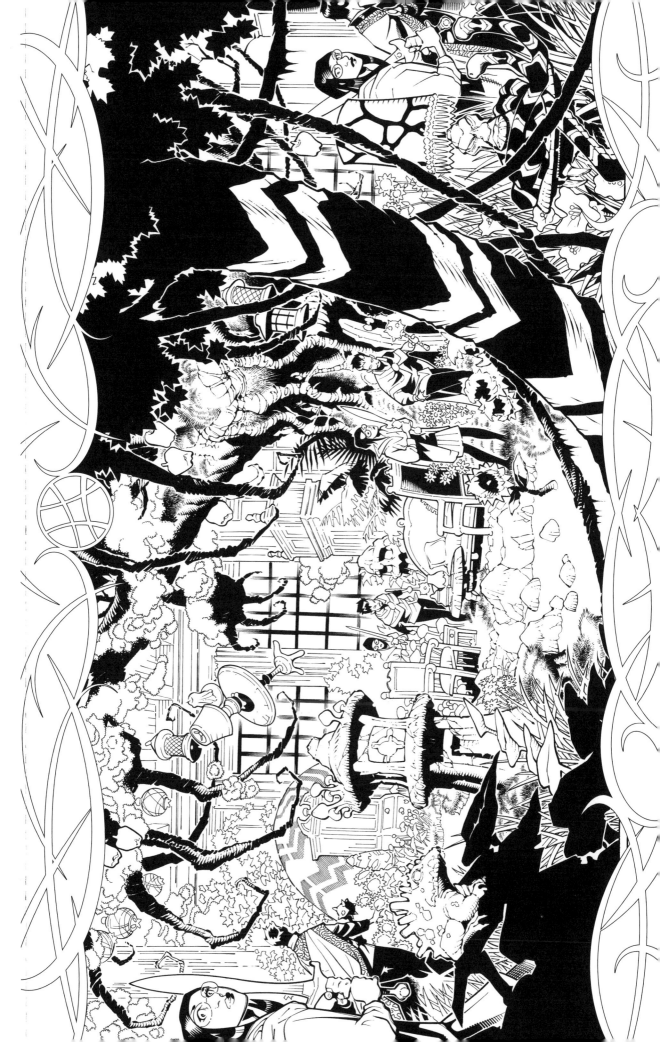

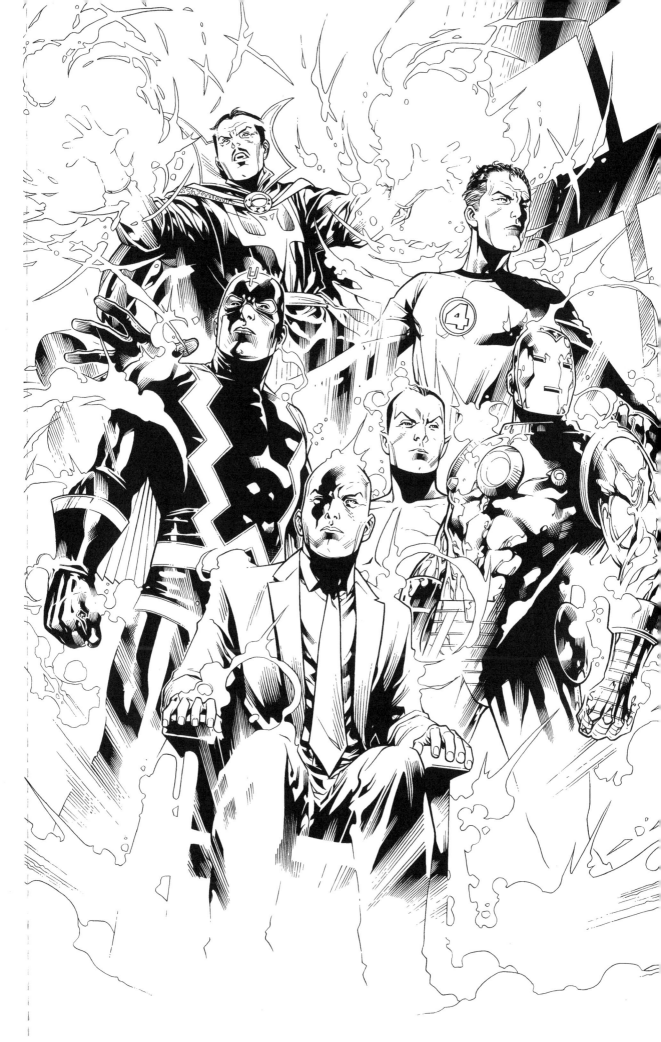

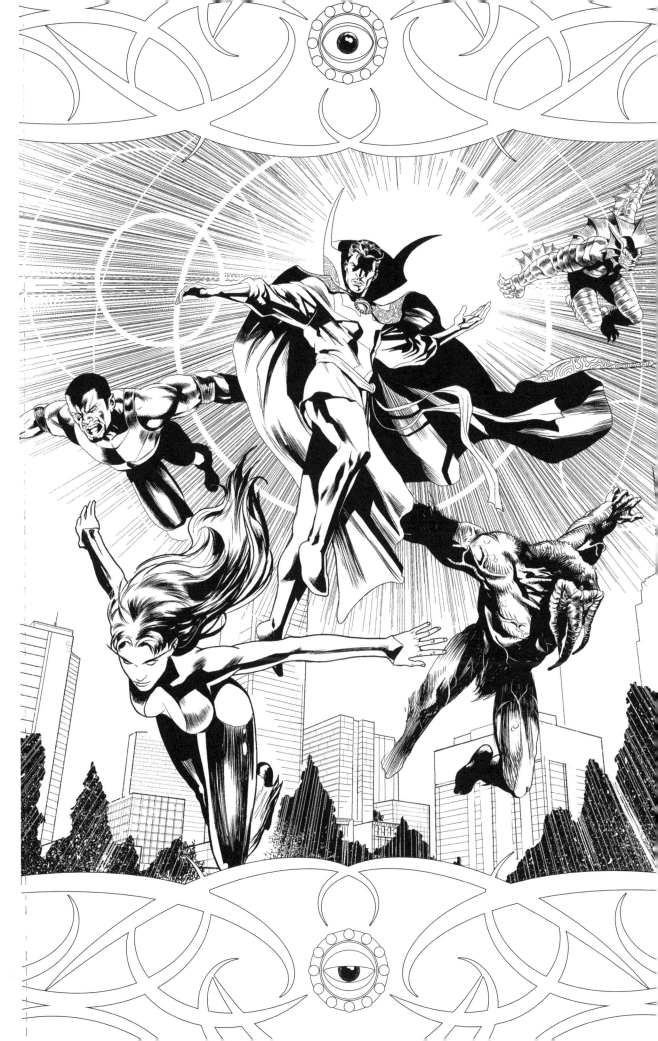

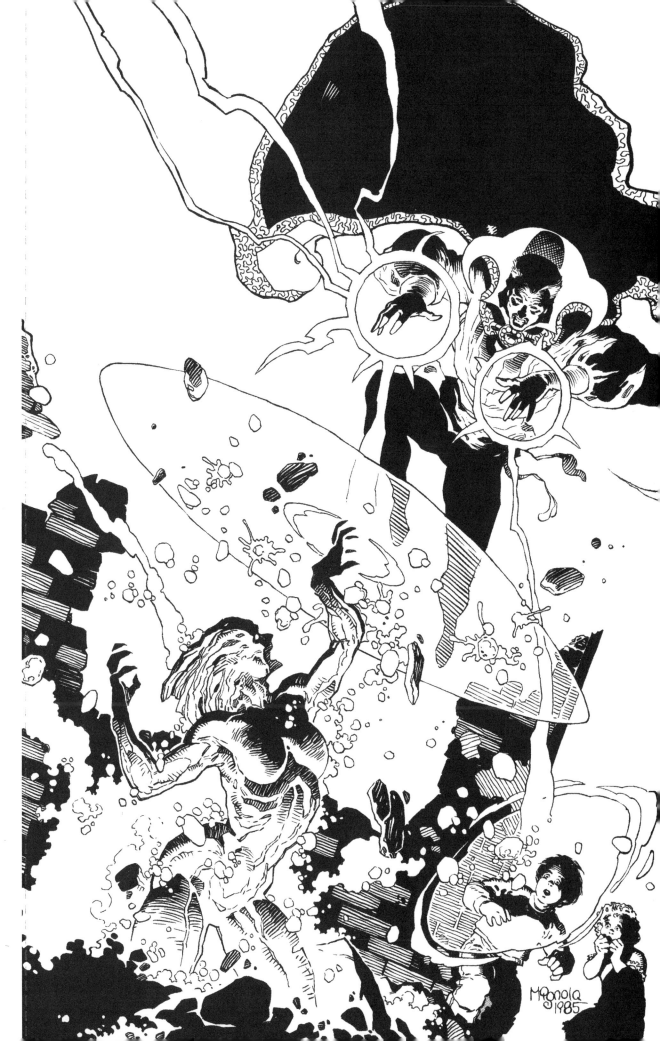

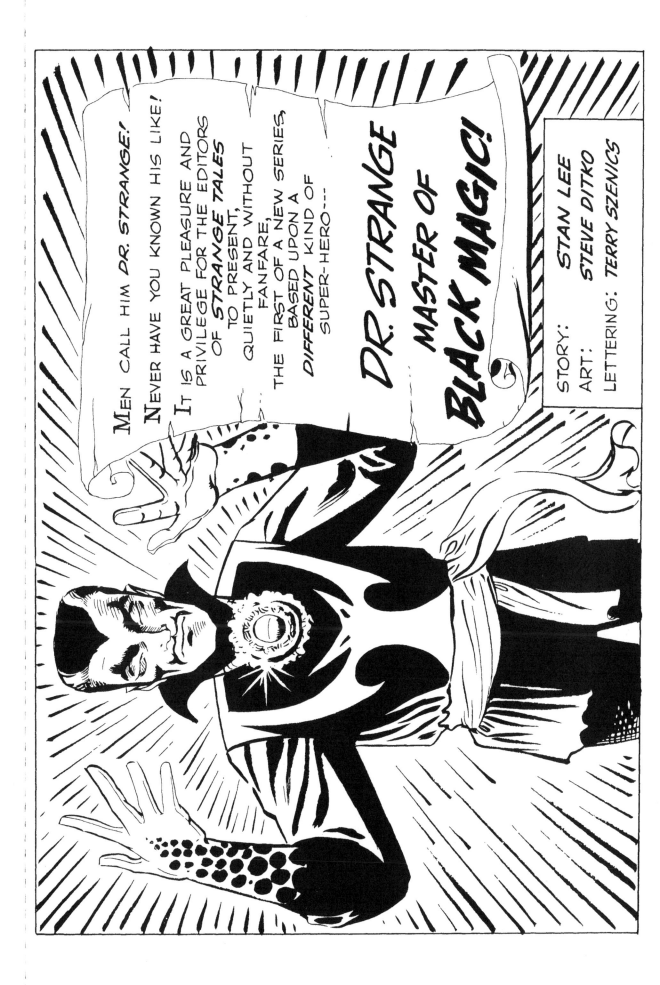

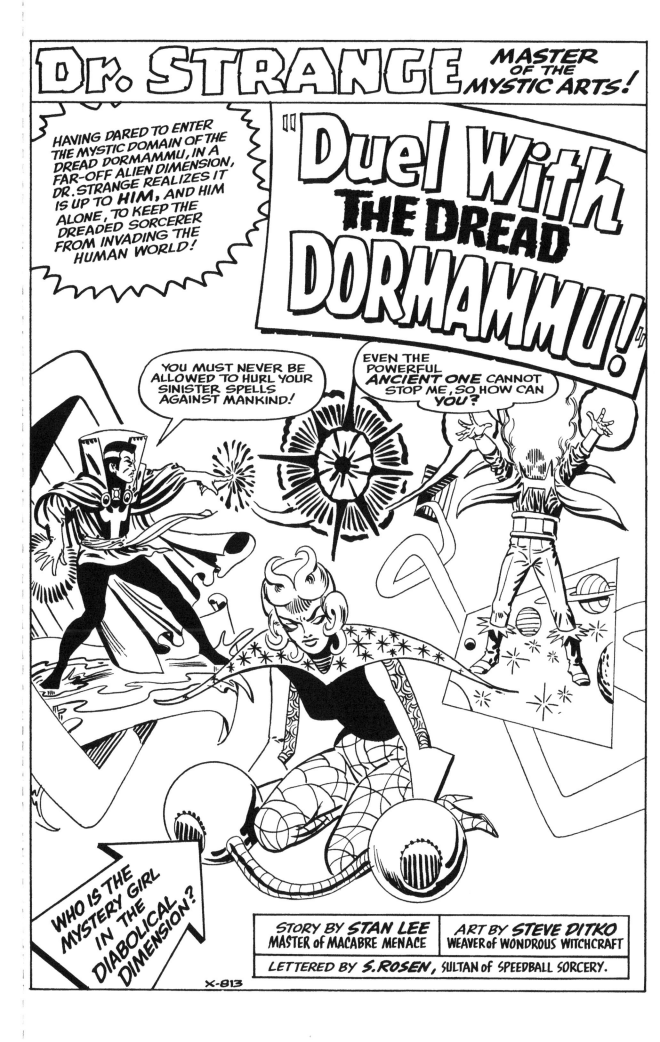

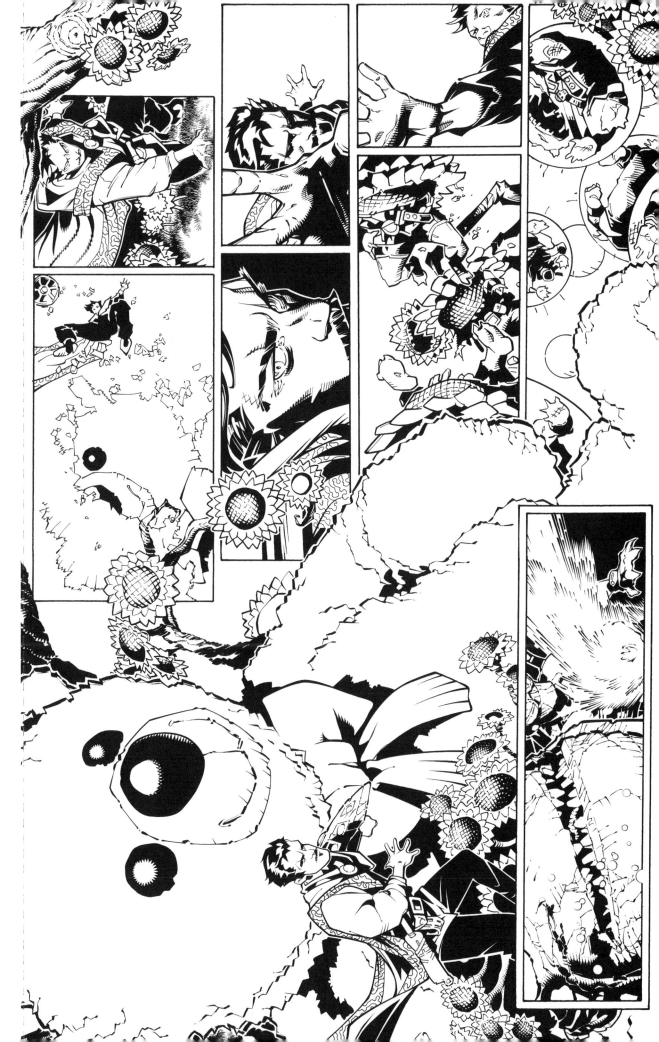

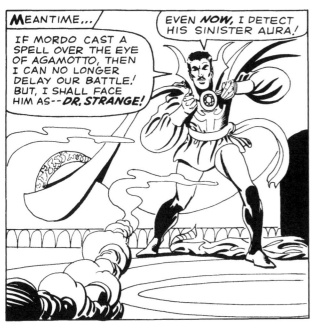

MEANTIME...

IF MORDO CAST A SPELL OVER THE EYE OF AGAMOTTO, THEN I CAN NO LONGER DELAY OUR BATTLE! BUT, I SHALL FACE HIM AS--*DR. STRANGE!*

EVEN *NOW*, I DETECT HIS SINISTER AURA!

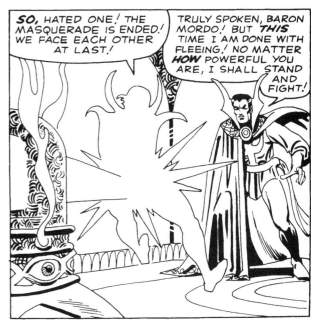

SO, HATED ONE! THE MASQUERADE IS ENDED! WE FACE EACH OTHER AT LAST!

TRULY SPOKEN, BARON MORDO! BUT *THIS* TIME I AM DONE WITH FLEEING! NO MATTER *HOW* POWERFUL YOU ARE, I SHALL STAND AND FIGHT!

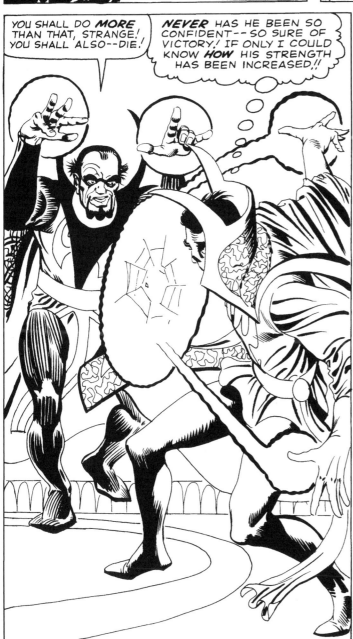

YOU SHALL DO *MORE* THAN THAT, STRANGE! YOU SHALL ALSO--*DIE!*

NEVER HAS HE BEEN SO CONFIDENT--SO SURE OF VICTORY! IF ONLY I COULD KNOW *HOW* HIS STRENGTH HAS BEEN INCREASED!!

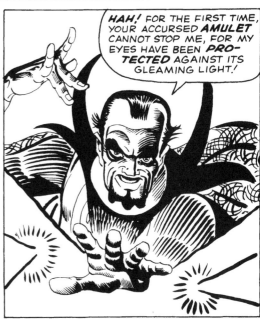

HAH! FOR THE FIRST TIME, YOUR ACCURSED *AMULET* CANNOT STOP ME, FOR MY EYES HAVE BEEN *PROTECTED* AGAINST ITS GLEAMING LIGHT!

SPELL AFTER SPELL IS HURLED AT DR. STRANGE--SPELLS WITHOUT LIMIT-- WITHOUT END-- FOR THE SOURCE OF MORDO'S POWER COMES FROM A FAR DISTANT DIMENSION!

HE'S BATTERING ME UNMERCI- FULLY! HOW MUCH LONGER CAN I HOLD OUT??

7

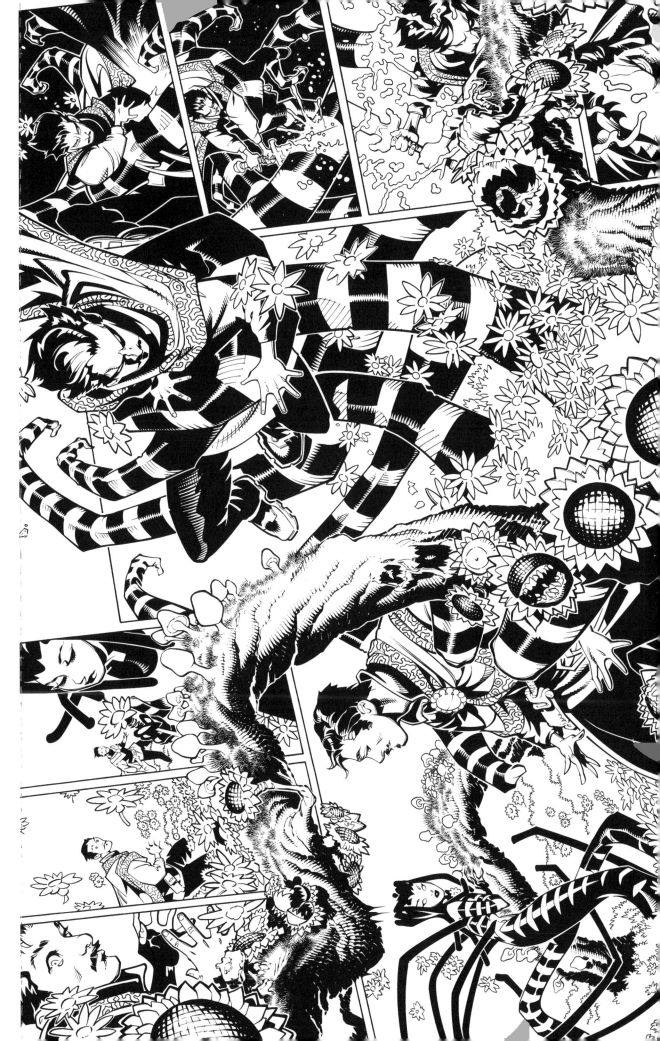

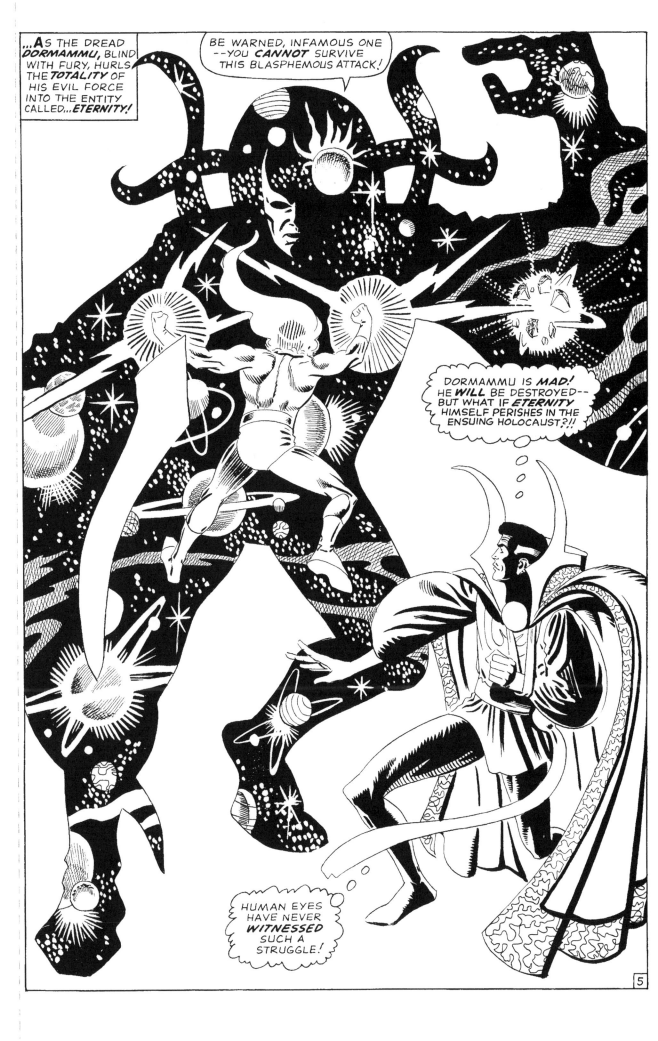

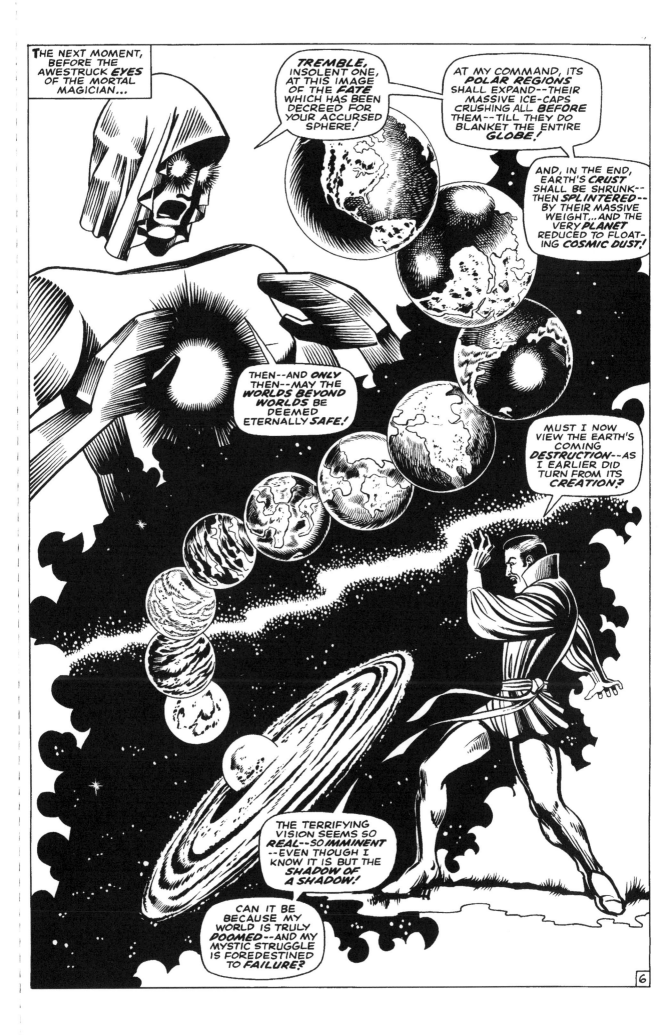

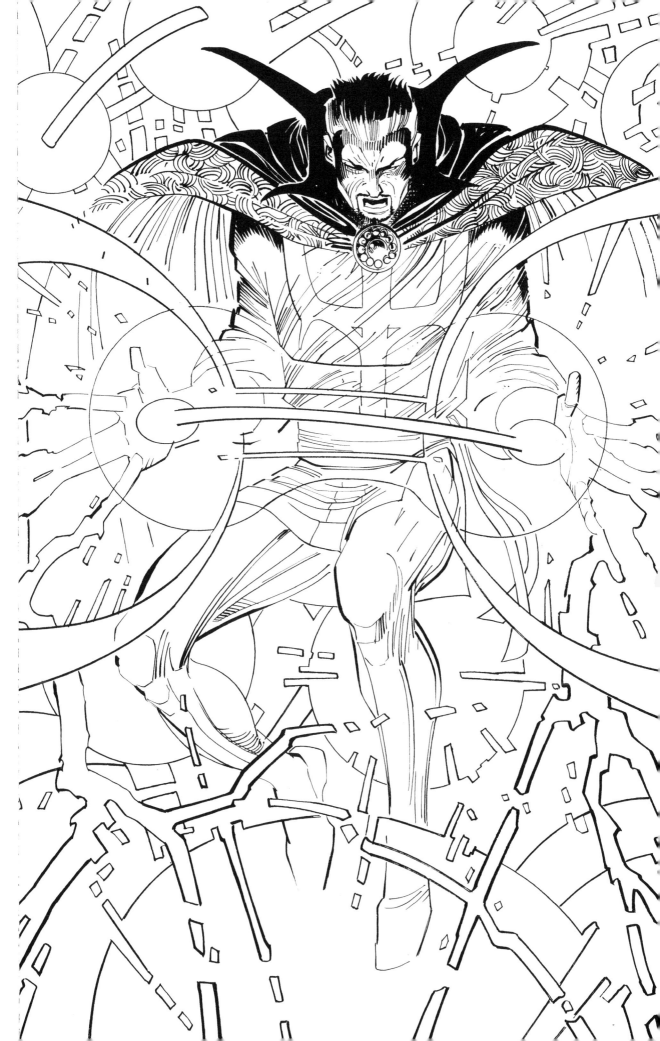

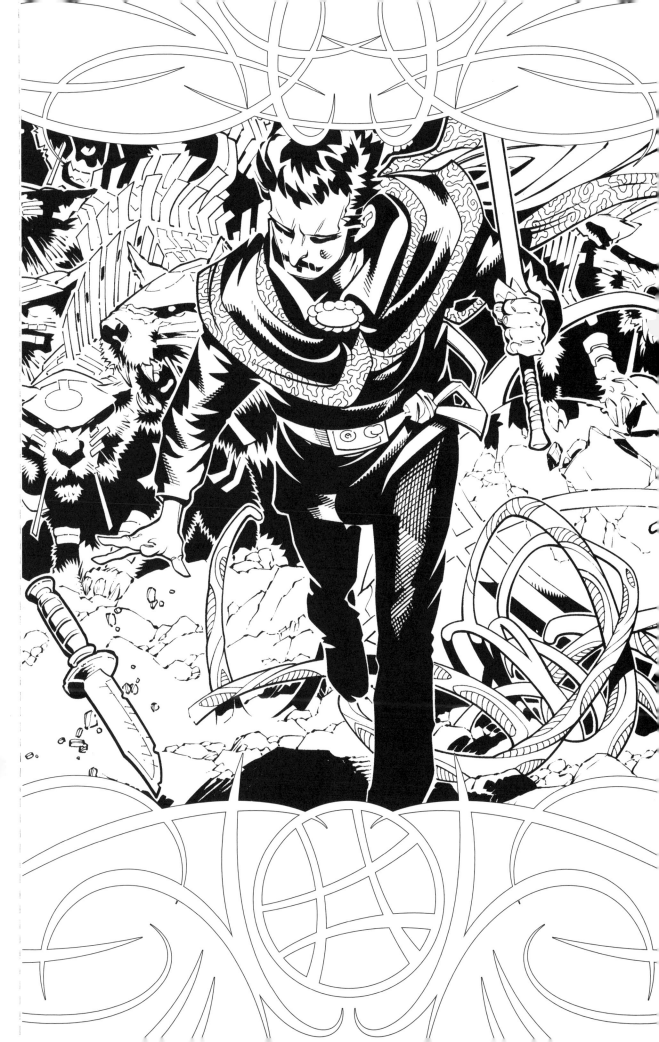